LIVES OF MODERN WOMEN

General Editor: Emma Tennant

Freya Stark

Caroline Moorehead

VIKING

VIKING
Penguin Books Ltd, Harmondsworth, Middlesex, England
Viking Penguin Inc., 40 West 23rd Street, New York, New York 10010, U.S.A.
Penguin Books Australia Ltd, Ringwood, Victoria, Australia
Penguin Books Canada Ltd, 2801 John Street, Markham, Ontario, Canada L3R 1B4
Penguin Books (N.Z.) Ltd, 182–190 Wairau Road, Auckland 10, New Zealand

First published 1985
Published simultaneously in Penguins

Copyright © Caroline Moorehead, 1985

Made and printed in Great Britain by
Richard Clay (The Chaucer Press) Ltd,
Bungay, Suffolk
Set in Monophoto Photina

British Library Cataloguing in Publication Data available
Moorehead, Caroline
  Freya Stark.—(Lives of modern women)
  1. Stark, Freya   2. Orientalists—Biography
  I. Title   II. Series
  910.4'092'4   DS61.7.S83

ISBN 0-670-80675-7

or 13.95/7.56 – 7/86

For Daniel

CONTENTS

LIST OF MAPS

1893	31 January, born in Paris, first daughter of Robert and Flora Stark.
1893–1900	Chagford, Devon, where her father built four houses along the edge of Dartmoor.
1901	Moved with her mother and younger sister Vera to northern Italy, first to Asolo, then Dronero.
1912–14	Bedford College, University of London, reading history.
1914–18	Briefly a censor, then a nurse, ending up with the George Trevelyan Ambulance Unit near Gorizia, Italy.
1926	Death of Vera.
1927	Departure for the East.
1930–31	Travels in Persia and the Near East.
1932–3	On the staff of the *Baghdad Times*. Publication of *Baghdad Sketches*. Awarded the Back Grant for her travels in Luristan.
1934	Publication of *The Valleys of the Assassins*. Awarded the Burton Memorial Medal.
1935–8	Travels in the Hadhramaut. Publication of *The Southern Gates of Arabia; Seen in the Hadhramaut*.
1939–40	Assistant Information Officer in Aden.

CHRONOLOGY

1940–43	Setting up the Brotherhood of Freedom in Cairo and Baghdad.
1942	Awarded the Royal Geographical Society's Founder's Medal.
1945	Assistant to Lady Wavell, Vicereine of India, in Delhi.
1947	Marriage to Stewart Perowne.
1948	Publication of *Perseus in the Wind*, a first selection of essays.
1950	Publication of *Traveller's Prelude*, the first of four volumes of autobiography.
1952–65	Main travels in Asia Minor. Publication of books of travel and history, including *Ionia: a Quest*, *Alexander's Path* and *Rome on the Euphrates*.
1972	Made Dame of the British Empire.
1974–82	Publication of eight volumes of letters.

ACKNOWLEDGEMENTS

The first acknowledgement must of course go to Dame Freya Stark, on whose autobiography and many letters, both published and unpublished, I have drawn repeatedly.

Next, to Mr Teddy Hodgkin and Mr Jock Murray, who gave me invaluable help with both research and correction, and to Mr Wilfrid Blunt, for permission to see an unpublished biographical notebook kept by Sir Sydney Cockerell.

I would also like to thank, for their time, patience and memories: Miss Lulie Abul Huda, Viscount and Viscountess Boyd, Lord David Cecil, Sybil, Marchioness of Cholmondeley, Mr and Mrs Nigel Clive, Mr and Mrs Derek Cooper, Mrs Lavender Goddard-Wilson, Mrs Peggy Hackforth-Jones, Mr John Hemming, Mr William Henderson, Mr Derek Hill, Mrs Doreen Ingrams, Sir Laurence Kirwan, Mrs Barclay Larsson, Mr Mark Lennox-Boyd, Professor and Mrs Lloyd, Mrs Catriona Luckhurst, Viscount Norwich, Mr Stewart Perowne, Signora Caroly Piaser, Mr Michael Russell, Mr Malise Ruthven, Mr Anthony Sheil, Miss Emma Tennant, Mr Colin Thubron, Mr Richard Waller and Mr Gordon Waterfield.

CHAPTER ONE

Dartmoor and Dronero

'The beckoning counts, and not the clicking latch behind you: and all through life the actual moment of emancipation still holds that delight, of the whole world coming to meet you like a wave.' Freya Stark was fifty-six when she wrote those words, in the first volume of her autobiography, *Traveller's Prelude*; she was referring to an incident shortly before her fourth birthday, when she set out from her Dartmoor home for Plymouth, with a mackintosh, a toothbrush and a penny, intent on finding a ship and putting out to sea. By four she was a practised traveller, having been carried at a very early age, long before the turn of the century, in a basket over the Dolomites to Cortina, and crossing regularly between her father's Devonshire moors and the European cities of her mother's family.

Whether travellers are formed by early voyages is hard to say. For Freya there was never a moment of turning back: well into her nineties, the beckoning continued to count, the clicking latch meant only the joy of being on the move again, to observe and listen, and then to put on paper something of the pleasure of remote places and of their past. It is as a traveller, more than historian, archaeologist or scholar that she is known: self-disciplined, courageous, ruthless as most true travellers are, with largely self-taught knowledge and a sense of leisure and concern for morality that ties her firmly to a vanished world.

Very few independent women have been greatly fond of Empire, for by and large they have got little from it. Freya, admirer of soldiers, upholder of tradition, full of intelligent appraisal of what it had to offer, is one of the great exceptions to prove the rule. She was not a great explorer for, by the time she travelled to the East, the age of exploration was over; nor a distinguished Arabist, in the way that Sir Ronald Storrs was; nor an exceptionally scholarly historian: but she is an extraordinary figure, perhaps because so relentless with herself.

Freya is of the same mould as Isabella Bird or Flora Lewis, though of course coming later, but she is of their time, by upbringing, conviction and purpose. However obvious the comparison, it is still tempting to liken her to Gertrude Bell. Both were Arabists and came to Arabia late; both were full of contradictions – the one rather manly, the other always feminine, loving hats; both possessed characters of steel. Though Freya never had Gertrude Bell's wealth, nor her power, for Bell was possibly one of the most powerful women in the British Empire for the few years before she died, she has her drive, her strength, her enduring curiosity. 'The true wanderer, whose travels are happiness,' she wrote when she was seventy-five, 'goes out not to shun, but to seek.' Freya has been a wanderer all her life.

*

Freya's parents were first cousins. There was a grand-mother in Torquay, a small and fragile woman who wore black ruffly silks and for whom the Victorian sense of order might have been invented. The house was all chintz and mahogany, velvet and bric-à-brac, with a 'sort of sacredness of tradition and routine . . . Every morning at eleven a sponge finger would be given us out of a silver box; every day at teatime a saucer of milk would be handed to the cat.' Even the animals seemed never to change, a yellow cat being succeeded by an identical younger beast, then an-other, without apparent break. It was a life of tranquillity, security and some money, but no excessive regard for it, in which people took time to talk and listen and, when they could, to travel.

The other grandmother, on Freya's mother's side, lived in an apartment in Genoa, a more robust and formidable figure, with square face, greenish-grey eyes and a mouth 'neither pinched nor mean, but obstinate, with apparently an equal capacity for turning hard or gentle, according to the vicissitudes of life'. The Genoa grandmother had known more affluent days. As the daughter of a court painter in Aix-la-Chapelle, married to a well-to-do English artist who had seen her as she took the air in an open carriage in the Corso in Rome, she had presided over a Florentine salon where the Brownings, Thackerays and Trollopes had all been guests, until her husband was bitten by a mad dog and died in his early forties, leaving her with four daughters.

One of these was Flora, tall, with red-gold curls and a buoyant confidence born of life in a sunny Tuscan villa. She was seventeen when Robert Stark, a sculptor with country tastes, eight years older, brought her back to the isolated English moors he loved. Flora had never been to England. The journey itself was severe: after Newton Abbot a shabby country train with metal foot-warmers for the next stage to Moretonhampstead, then a pony carriage for the final seven-mile drive among the turnips. Towards the end, the track rose into the remote barrenness of treeless fields and boulders, with runnels of water trickling through the turf. There was no tarmac. An English countrywoman might have let her spirits fall. For a girl made for the 'easy, cultured, gregarious surface life of the South' the prospect of happiness seemed dim indeed. Flora, Freya wrote later, was 'singularly ill-equipped to deal with the Victorian order so uncompromisingly superimposed on the untidiness of God'.

Robert Stark walked, rode and began building what were to be four stone and granite houses. The first was Scorhill, on a steep slope above the North Teign where Dartmoor ends and the woods begin. The last was Ford Park, with an Italianate veranda and wooden balcony, and flint-granite windows, set hard up against the mountain. Inside, the rooms were beamed and wood panelled. From the upper windows you could see the piled rocks of Middle Tor and Kestor, and, nearer, the rare shrubs and trees which were his real passion. On his orders, and often by his own hand, lakes were scooped out of dips in the moor and glades of azaleas, rhododendrons and bamboos planted. Much is still there: the gardens now overgrown and dense, and from the moor itself the natural lie of the land looks almost distorted, so heavy and almost alien are his woods encroaching upon it.

In the 1880s there was no electricity; peat gave out a pale heat from the narrow Victorian fireplaces. It was cold beyond belief. Several weeks each year the moorland houses were cut off by snowdrifts from Chagford, twenty minutes away by horse. When the snow ended, it rained. With three times the rainfall of the Southern Counties, Dartmoor seemed to drip, perpetually sodden. There was little to do but walk or ride. One afternoon Robert came home to find the house shuttered up, the lamps and candles lit and Flora reading, with desperate intensity. The south-west wind had been blowing ceaselessly for three days; she had walked or ridden morning and afternoon until there were no more dry tweeds. Then she had given up.

The Starks had been married thirteen years before Freya, their first surviving child, was born in Paris on 31 January 1893. Even so, her arrival was unexpected, for she came at seven months 'in the middle of Bohemia . . . with not a garment ready to receive me', so that Robert Stark and a student painter friend, Herbert Young, had to hasten off to the Galeries Lafayette for some clothes. It was one of the rare periods of harmony in the Stark marriage. Both Robert and Flora were good painters, (a rhinoceros sculpted by him is in the Tate); Flora had been studying at Julien's atelier in Paris and had not long before received a medal for a picture in the Salon. She had learnt to ride a bicycle, wearing bloomers. A year later came a second daughter, Vera.

Frequent moves made Flora's life just tolerable. There were escapes to London, where she played the piano and was invited into the St John's Wood artists' circle. There were nearly three years in a drab small villa in Farnham, so very preferable to the wet moors, and there were many expeditions to Genoa. The girls had governesses, most memorably a German girl who sang songs to them in the firelight sitting on the floor, and wore blue-and-white striped cotton blouses. Later came la Contessina, of impoverished Italian nobility, whom they loved and trampled on. Vera, with thick pigtails and pink cheeks, was good; Freya, a 'sort of byword for naughtiness'. Despite the governesses the girls remained wild, little educated and without other companions. They wore long ribbed woollen stockings, and got holes in them. They climbed trees. On Dartmoor, there were occasional 'appalling social picnics', with footmen handing out sandwiches, from which they fled like rabbits. Robert and Flora were seldom happy any longer. Freya was never to forget 'the sight of my mother's grim expression, doing the housework she hated', nor her father's mute and wistful unassumingness; observing their distress left her with an enduring hatred of argument.

In 1901 came a break. Flora took the girls to Asolo, the village in the foothills of the Dolomites where Robert Browning's son Pen, a friend from student days, had bought and restored three houses, and where Herbert Young had now settled in a gatehouse in the village walls. Asolo was a charming place, and it is largely unaltered today: in the lee of a hill, on which lay scattered a few stone remains of a pre-Roman fortress, it had a square with trees and a fountain with a pedestal in the form of a fat Venetian lion squatting on its haunches. The narrow streets were lined with crooked and irregular porticoes. It was here that Catherine Cornaro, last Queen of Cyprus, kept a lively and provincial court, when the Venetian grandees brought her from her island, and it was Bembo, her Cardinal, who invented the word 'asolare' to describe the 'purposeless, leisurely, agreeable passing of time'.

Herbert Young was greatly attached to the two little girls. He read them Malory. In 1903 came a move to Dronero, a grey and cobbled town in a valley in Piedmont, drawn there by a new friend of Flora's, Count Mario di Roascio, a short, round young man who wore his moustache dipping downwards and who was starting a carpet business. Flora had taken La Mal Pensa, which had a garden full of glass pavilions and summer houses and a pond of croaking frogs. Robert Stark stayed behind in Chagford, though he came out to Italy for occasional holidays, when he taught the girls cricket and bought them guinea pigs with which they practised 'power politics with a fierce guinea pig, a bully, and a very timid one which my father would pick up and push towards the Dictator'. One year they went to Le Touquet and tobogganed down the sand dunes.

La Mal Pensa was too cold for winters. Flora and the two girls moved into part of a great house in the town, which was still icy, with marble, tessellated floors, then, the following year, into a fine old whitewashed villa away in the vineyards on the slope of a hill. The plain lay below them, and thirty miles away they could see the Bismarda, a peak covered most of the year in snow. Freya and Vera were sent off to the nuns at the Sacré Cœur convent every day to learn French and embroidery. The family were not well off. There was little money for wood and rarely butter or jam for breakfast. More painfully, a haze of scandal was building up

over their heads: Flora had become increasingly involved in
Mario Roascio's factory and people now assumed that he
had become her lover. The girls felt shame and confusion;
Freya, the elder, took on the role of leader, self-reliant, rather
judging, perhaps, with a concern for morality and behaviour
that was not to leave her. Vera remained passive.

Mario was quarrelsome, jealous and dictatorial; he discouraged all friendships and the visitors who did come
usually left after some disagreeable exchange. 'I am glad to
say', wrote Freya somewhat stuffily many years later, 'that
Vera and I kept our sense of proportion . . . Work was the
household god and only people who worked like ourselves
were any good at all.'

For by now Freya, aged thirteen, had found out about
books. She was reading French, a lot of Dumas, and beginning to teach herself Latin. The desire to study had come
to her on a summer visit to Chagford, when the un-
accustomed heat had brought honeysuckle out all over Ford
Park, the pond had been full of red and white water lilies
and the girls bathed early each morning in the waterfalls.
While the others played tennis on a court covered in
molehills and later went cubbing and hunting, Freya read
'those books which come in one's life as a landscape
suddenly revealed, a turning point which never again leaves
one'. There was Plato's dialogue on the death of Socrates,
which seemed to her to answer every question about the
future of the spirit; there was the life of Darwin, and the
Origin of the Species; there were Milton, Spenser and Hazlitt,
picked at random from the shelves. Before they returned to
Dronero that winter, Freya read the whole of Caesar's wars

from beginning to end with the help of a dictionary. It was to be one of her longest and most fondly remembered visits to Dartmoor, for Robert Stark had decided to start a new life farming in Canada, and now sold Ford Park to the Duchy of Cornwall. Before he left, he and Freya paced out seven acres of moorland to give to her where the 'hills faded into one another to a far distance'. Along one side ran a stream, for fishing; the rest, a sloping hillside of turf, they marked with boulders. They stand there still, an 'S' clearly carved into the rock.

It was fortunate that Freya had learned the pleasure of books; they gave her a new anchor, a discipline, a longing to see and discover the world, and they opened a line of doors that would go on opening forever. At this moment in particular, however, their appeal was vital. One afternoon she went to visit the new factory Mario had opened in Dronero where, standing by the vast looms, her long hair hanging almost to her knees, she was suddenly caught up in one of the steel shafts and carried round, her feet striking the wall as she was dragged by. When she was pulled out, half her scalp was found to have been torn away. It was four months before she left hospital, patched up by the then totally new invention of skin grafts, but forever slightly disfigured down one side of her face. It was the sort of accident to break the confidence of any young girl; Freya, resilient already, became more so. Overcoming it added to her enormous natural courage, and gave her physical and mental reserves she later had need of; but the accident also made her very vulnerable in all things to do with her appearance and her effect on other people.

In 1908 Freya was allowed to stay on her own in London, at the house of Viva Jeyes and her husband Harry, assistant editor of the *Standard*, one of the evening papers, a sensible and brilliant man who talked about politics and books with her while they exercised the dogs in Regents Park. She met W. P. Ker, later Professor of Poetry at Oxford and one of the most distinguished literary men of his time, and started going to his lectures in English at London University. He was unusually well loved, his students showing their approval by a gentle stamping of feet when he arrived in the lecture hall. Freya considered him her adopted godfather and said that he taught her all she knew of English literature, correcting her essays by writing underneath 'too many words'.

For the next few years her frequent stays in London were to provide both great pleasure and great doubt. She delighted in the work, which by 1912 had become a degree course at Bedford College; she enjoyed the few literary soirées to which she was invited – there was one dinner with Yeats, Sickert and Edmund Gosse – and she took a certain anxious enjoyment in some new dresses. But she felt herself to be unattractive, over and above her scarred face, in the mannish shirts and unbecoming suits of the day, and podgy with a nose that was too big. She had also become shy, believing that her fellow students found her elaborate Italian manners affected. Rather than join them for lunch, she ate pâté sandwiches in a French café. She was at her happiest listening to W. P. Ker, or discussing the week's *Nation* and *Spectator* with Herbert Young, or, when returning to Dartmoor to stay with friends, talking socialism with a new acquaintance called Dorothy, as they raced their ponies along the Druid avenues and circles of the moor. Dorothy wanted to be a sanitary inspector.

In Dronero, pleasure came only when she and Vera escaped to walk in the mountains, or when Mario could be persuaded to let Flora and her daughters go off without him. To the girls, their mother seemed always too ready to placate him, to make sacrifices for him she would not make for them. 'My mother asked too much,' Freya wrote in *Traveller's Prelude*, 'and later on it was hard to forgive.' These years set the tone for her often ambivalent relationship with her mother: yearning, as if never receiving quite enough affection, and trying to win more, yet also slightly censorious, which made her ever after the custodian of family morals. By now, whenever in Italy, she was put in charge of the housekeeping, and at forty lire a month in wages she was being schooled to run the factory office. It took her nearly a year to notice that Mario was courting her, a suppressed unsettling courtship from which she backed sharply away. Three years later, Mario married Vera, who, having agreed to become a Catholic, spent the night before the ceremony crying in Freya's arms.

Both wars had an exceptionally strong effect on Freya's life and outlook; from both she emerged more resolute, more established, more appreciated. But she cannot be said to have approached the first war unformed. In 1914 she was twenty-one, a 'very funny little thing', according to friends, in the home-made dresses she wore very long, after Flora told her that long clothes suited short people better than short ones. She spoke English with a slight foreign accent, and had completed most stages of an honours degree at London University, not in English but in History, saying that 'I found the former meant too much reading *about* people while for history one spent one's time with the sources themselves.'

She was, she thought, 'pretty tough' after her wandering life, and in total control of her temper, having simply decided, at the age of twelve, watching her mother's bouts of violent rage, that she would never let it become uncontrolled. She was not proud, 'due always, I believe ... to a genuine love of inquiry into things for their own sake'. And most surprising of all, perhaps, she was not bitter, drawing strength from the 'warmth and affection' of her Dartmoor early childhood, from the honesty of her father from whom she considered that she had inherited a 'feeling of almost physical discomfort in the face of any lie which has lasted through life' and from her mother's vitality, if not her constancy.

She could ride, dance, embroider, construe Latin, speak perfect Italian and adequate French and German. And she had the memory of a landscape, 'so that I never move into Devonshire lanes or towards the Dartmoor tors without the knowledge that my roots are there', that she was later to carry with her to the not dissimilar flat, undulating, green pastures of Luristan.

CHAPTER TWO

The First World War

Whatever the immediate appeal of more ambitious and distant travel, Freya was not now to get away for another thirteen years. Five were taken up by the war; after that, there was still much to settle and much to learn for a young woman in her twenties of Victorian background.

As news came of the fighting she decided to abandon all further education and left to train as a nurse at the clinic of St Ursula in Bologna. She lodged with acquaintances in a palazzo and was chaperoned by an elderly English governess. Freya was the first respectable woman to volunteer: the other nurses were prostitutes who spent their evenings pursuing their other profession. They were envious of Freya and not very friendly.

As a nurse, she was capable and diligent and made queasy solely by the operating theatre, though the only occasion she actually fainted was when she gave an overdose of anaesthetic to a woman with a weak heart who almost died. She came round to find a young doctor leaning over her: 'You shouldn't get so agitated, signorina. We have all killed somebody.' It soon fell to Freya to protect the doctors from the do-gooding Italian Red Cross ladies who, as the war spread, thronged the hospital corridors in their pearls and emerald clasps, worn prominently over their nursing aprons.

Away from the hospital, the old families of Bologna continued to behave as if there were no European war. They took Freya to the opera and for picnics in the Apennines. In her lunch hours she read the war news in the sedate *Resto del Carlino*; one day, in error, she was given *Popolo d'Italia*. In it she found an article by a Benito Mussolini. It was, she noted, most impressive.

The brother of the friend who had introduced her into the clinic was a bacteriologist called Guido Rueta, a tall young man with a small, pointed beard. By Christmas he was calling every day, with flowers and books. From behind her partition, the English governess did her best to chaperone, setting off her alarm clock when she judged the hour had come for Guido to leave. In the New Year, he proposed. He was thirty-eight; Freya just twenty-two. 'Most people luckily have the short and perfect happiness of such a time in their lives,' Freya wrote in a long letter nearly thirty years later, 'when every trivial moment lives as if in a halo of its own.' Freya's time lasted nearly a year. In the spring they went to visit Guido's family in Perugia, choosing a moment when the anemones were out.

By early summer, Freya appeared to be getting thinner and thinner. Flora hated illness and now, as when a child, Freya did her best to suppress all symptoms. After some weeks, typhoid was diagnosed, soon complicated by pleurisy and then pneumonia. Her temperature rose to 107. She was haunted by a strange terror of certain colours. The battle of Verdun was being fought; the horror of it wandered through her dreams.

Guido had by now been put in charge of the disinfecting and reassembling of equipment collected on the battlefields, and had been promised a more permanent post as director of a clinic in Salsomaggiore. In May a letter came breaking off the engagement. He gave no reason. Only later did Freya learn that before meeting her he had lived for many years with a musician who had left him and gone to America. Hearing of Freya, and the new job, she hastened back and they married a year later.

When Freya was well enough she escaped her mother, whose disappointment over the broken engagement had taken the form of petty niggling over the furniture and presents exchanged between the couple, and returned to find solace in England, 'in every light and line of the land'. Immediately she looked for work. Viva Jeyes was running an all-night sandwich-and-coffee stall at Paddington Station. Freya went to help as trainloads of Australian troops, bound for the Somme and singing 'Tipperary' rumbled in. To Flora in Dronero she wrote sternly: 'I feel that it doesn't matter what one does or what happens so long as we bear it properly and do not lose our sense of proportion or throw up the sponge and be miserable just because we are one of a few million who are going through a bad time.'

While waiting to nurse again – she had applied for more training at the Hornsey Cottage Hospital – she worked in the Censor's office reading letters in French, German and Italian, and complaining that when the weather grew cold

120 of her allotted 150 letters contained references to burst pipes. It was, however, a skill and it was to be extremely useful to her in the second war. 'It developed that sort of sixth sense for what people are *really* meaning, which the whole of intelligence or propaganda work is built on.' She became extremely adept at spotting spies. When she could get away she wrote poems in the British Museum and took tea or dinner with W. P. Ker in his house in Gower Street, lit only by candles, and where books lined every room from floor to ceiling. She was rather jealous of his other, proper, god-daughters.

In the early autumn of 1917 the historian G. M. Trevelyan's ambulance unit was based in the Villa Trento, an old Venetian villa ten miles from Gorizia with outbuildings which were used as repair shops for the ambulances and a vast granary that had been turned into two wards, Garibaldi and Aosta, the last named after the famous duchess who was organizing nurses for the field hospitals. The villa had been set up by a former doctor at the Rome Embassy who saw it as a centre and a symbol of Anglo-Italian friendship. Because of her fluent Italian, Freya was despatched here, with a rank equivalent to lieutenant for her train journey with the troops across Europe.

The first month was peaceful. Freya washed in a tin basin and made beds. She shared a painted room with four other VADs and worried about letting disinfectant fall through the floorboards into the wine vats below. To Flora, to whom she wrote regularly, as she was now to do until her mother's death thirty years later, she reported a little sadly: 'I haven't any young men friends.'

By October the war was coming closer. In the battle for Monte San Gabriele there were hundreds of casualties on both sides; it was a 'gruesome slaughter house' with little shelter for the troops. From the hills above Villa Trento the nurses watched the fighting, a front that weaved and recoiled like a snake through the vineyards. The shelling made the windows rattle.

On 24 October two divisions of enemy troops broke through at Caporetto, and the retreat began. On the 28th, Freya noted in her diary that they had been travelling for twenty and a half hours, frequently stuck in heavy rain and persistent winds. 'The retreat looks like a panic; Udine evacuated; wounded trudging in the rain.' Along the side of the road lay dead horses; lorries and men shuffled through shuttered streets. The unit reached Padua on the 30th; their stores and kit had gone and twenty of their thirty-five cars had been lost. The intention had been to re-form and continue the hospital; the order now came for the unit to go '*in riposo*'. Freya, no longer needed, made her way back to Dronero.

Shortly after Armistice Day, Robert Stark returned to Italy. The war years had not improved Flora's relations with Vera, over whose life and marriage she now seemed in complete, domineering control. With her father, Freya, more assertive than ever after five years of independence, formed a plan to buy a cottage some way from Piedmont, where Flora could be installed, and the three of them set off to wander along the now deserted coast of the Riviera. As they walked, Robert and Flora kept fifty yards apart.

They found what they wanted at La Mortola, not far from Ventimiglia and five minutes from the French border, in a small pebbly bay adjoining a property with famously beautiful water gardens. There was a vineyard, two and a half acres of land and a cottage with four little rooms, separated from the sea by the railway. The name of the property was L'Arma. It was peaceful and very beautiful.

The idea had been to provide some escape for Vera and also somewhere for her to bring her children. L'Arma also had to be made to pay. Freya had just over £90 a year to live on, her father having settled some capital on her; Flora, having sunk everything into Mario's factory, nothing. While Flora painted cupboards and dressers for the little house, Freya hauled water up the steep slopes and learned to prune the vines. One year she tried carnations and stocks, another, vegetables. In between fretting about the bills, she read the *Georgics*. Notebooks of the time contain dates for planting fruit trees, scraps of poetry, extracts from political speeches and recipes. In the summer evenings she would walk down the hill and swim out into the bay, where the fishermen caught anchovies and sardines by lamp-light. If sometimes lonely, she was also fully occupied and, whether consciously or not, schooling herself to develop a 'preference for this world as it is, and an inclination to deal with things one after another, even if they happen to be time and eternity'.

It was now that Freya became a smuggler, enjoying a talent and a nerve for it that was to give her considerable satisfaction and her friends considerable anxiety in the Middle Eastern years to come. A naval family nearby owned an early Sienese painting. A French collector saw it and offered £1,000 to its owner, and £100 to Freya, if she could get it to him. Freya borrowed a cart and pony, placed the masterpiece inside, seated a Scottish friend and her bags on top, and led the party over the border. Friends were later to call her, with affection, 'compulsively unscrupulous'; Freya, who saw no moral wickedness in them, relished such adventures.

After five years of war, Freya now rediscovered the mountains with W. P. Ker, her climbing companion since the early days of their friendship, but only for long days, not serious overnight mountaineering, for he declared that he loathed women climbers. In the immediate post-war years their expeditions became annual rituals, after which Freya would bring Ker back to L'Arma and force him to bathe, not as he always had, as an early-morning discipline, but as an agreeable social pastime. Friends, like Viva Jeyes, or Venetia Buddicom, now began to come regularly to stay, setting a pattern for visitors that has lasted all Freya's life.

In July 1923, at the start of what was to be a climb of Pizzo Bianco, 'W.P. gave a little sudden cry and died.' While the guide went for help, Freya sat with him for seven hours. He was buried in his old brown walking clothes, with a bunch of wild strawberries in his hand, in a cemetery he had liked, under the edge of Monte Rosa. Freya decided to climb again immediately, this time the Matterhorn, 'to get my strength again' in the solitude. She would miss him greatly, for friends were already of exceptional importance to her; but Freya was not sentimental: childhood, her accident, the war, Guido, had all combined to make her very adult for her years, and eager to become more so. 'I remember,' she wrote later, 'wishing often to find what might silence fear, and to reach the end of my days free from that mortal weakness.'

It was one of her last climbs. In the early twenties, Freya seemed permanently ailing. In the winter of 1924 doctors decided she had a gastric ulcer, and though an operation was successful, it was months before she was out of danger. Freya used these long periods of inactivity to master seventeenth-century embroidery and to learn Arabic, having decided, she told people later, that the 'most interesting things in the world were likely to happen in the neighbourhood of *oil*, and that was what really determined me'. (W. P. Ker, author of a scholarly book on the Edda legends, had urged her to take up Icelandic instead.)

People were later to doubt how truthful Freya was in her farsightedness. (At a dinner party in the sixties, Arthur Koestler told her that she was making it up. She replied that she was not accustomed to being contradicted. It was some time before they patched it up.) Whatever the case, Arabic was a considerable undertaking. Freya had found a white-bearded Capuchin in San Remo who had spent thirty years in Beirut and now bred Angora rabbits. Twice a week, she walked for an hour into Ventimiglia, caught a local train, and then walked a further couple of miles to the monastery. By 1922 she was reading the Koran. She was never easily put off anything.

For some years the family had been engaged in a lawsuit against Mario, in an attempt to recover some of the money put into his carpets (Freya won it). The unpleasantness meant that the two sisters met rarely. In 1926 Vera had a miscarriage; septicaemia developed. For two months she lived on, at times seeming about to recover. In August she died and was buried in the family vault near to the coffin of her small daughter Leonarda. 'I have known two great sorrows,' wrote Freya in *Traveller's Prelude*, 'the loss of Guido and of Vera . . . Vera's death is still as harsh as ever and will be as long as I can feel.'

Freya was now thirty-three and there was little to hold her in Europe; the time of travel could begin. Before she made her plans, however, Herbert Young wrote to ask her whether he might leave her his Asolo house, complete with furniture, as a place in which to live and not to sell, saying that he considered her the proper person to inherit this 'earthly paradise'. Freya accepted; she remembered with fondness the garden with its alley of over-arching hornbeams, the stone bacchus under the laurel tree, and, all over the back of the house, the rose 'Fortune's Yellow', the memory of which, she wrote during the Second World War, 'its rich bunches, nectarine coloured in a blue spring sky, come to me as a symbol of happiness'. Casa Freia, as the house was soon called, became the home round which her life and her journeys would revolve.

Furthermore, her income had at last risen to the desired sum of £300, brought about by a characteristic act of financial bravura on her part. A friend had written to tell her that Canadian Grand Trunk Railways shares were set to rise. She asked the manager of Barclay's Bank in Monte Carlo, who handled her money, to invest her entire capital in them. He protested, but was, as many were to be after him, courteously but firmly overruled. The shares dropped. When, a few days later, they rose spectacularly, Freya sold.

In June, Freya wrote to her father in Canada that she had met a Syrian Quaker who was going to find her a 'cheap lodging in an Arab village where I shall meet no Europeans'. Briefly tempted by the School of Oriental Studies in London and the classes of Sir Thomas Arnold and Sir Denison Ross (who used to hold the hands of pretty girls, 'but only did this once to me, for I was not at all pretty enough to be noticed'), she had decided instead to 'make for the real thing in Syria'. What was more, she was still unmarried, suitors having hovered and vanished, to the distress of her mother who felt that spinsterhood was a bad condition and who filled Freya with a conviction that 'it must be due to some invincible inferiority in myself'. What she needed now was to escape a 'miserable sense of being a failure'. Her health was still not good, but she had decided that she would rather die than endure the life of an invalid.

On 18 November 1927, feeling somewhat small and forlorn as she gazed up from the gondola bearing her and her luggage at the SS *Abbazia* spitting smoke and steam from its funnel in the port of Venice, having been baptized a Presbyterian, so as not to die 'outside the Christian brotherhood', she embarked 'for Beirut – and my travels in the East began'.

CHAPTER THREE

Travels in the East

By the middle of December, Freya was settled in a room in the village of Brummana in the Lebanon which, 'sung by Flecker, lay like a brown lizard on its ridge'. From the first days of departure, her spirits had risen, and they kept rising; it was all better, much better than she had hoped. Purposeful, self-contained, a woman alone spending little, she must have seemed strange to local people who were used to greater pomp and assertiveness among the few Europeans who had come this way. The bolder children crowded around her whenever she walked down the street while the men stared and the women followed her movements from behind shuttered windows. Everywhere, at all times, she was on show. Her response was simple. She acted calmly, with precision, and always pleasantly; she stopped to talk and ask questions, a parasol held over her head, in sensible suit and hat, or sat for hours sketching or just looking.

Freya was soon hard at work on her Arabic and setting a routine for daily life in the Middle East that was to remain a pattern for all her travels. She walked a good deal, making expeditions with a guide, having prepared herself well beforehand. She spent much time paying calls, sitting listening and practising Arabic; and she wrote letters, instructing her main correspondents to keep them, so that they would act as diary.

She had, as she herself recognized, one useful accomplishment: a true appreciation of leisure and the importance of not hurrying, but leaving time to listen and be accepted. It came, she felt, from early illnesses, and from the Victorian rules of her childhood, when dressing for dinner was customary and with it the 'casting away as it were of the day's business' so that she now felt herself most like the Arab nomad, 'who receives his world as it comes from Allah, and is not concerned to alter it more than he need'. She was soon completely charmed, the landscape and the people perfectly suited to her intense curiosity and strong sense of the romantic. 'I have been trying', she wrote, 'to think why it is all so fascinating, and have come to the conclusion that it is the feeling of a life not merely primitive – we have that in Italy – but genuinely wild . . . a feeling of the genuine original roughness of life.' To an English friend, she added: 'The East is getting a firm grip. What it is I don't know: not beauty, nor poetry, none of the usual things . . .'

There was better to come. In April, having moved from Brummana to Damascus, she looked at a map, picked out what seemed a lonely ruin, far from villages, and found a guide. To Penelope Ker, sister of W. P. Ker, she recorded her delight in what she had seen: 'Yesterday was a wonderful day: for I discovered the Desert! . . . Camels appeared on our left hand: first a few here and there, then more and more, till the whole herd came browsing along, five hundred or

more . . . Their huge legs rose up all around me like columns
. . . I stood in a kind of ecstasy among them . . . I never
imagined that my first sight of the desert would come as
such a shock of beauty and enslave me right away.'

Freya was neither the first nor the most remarkable of the
desert travellers, and indeed mountains, not deserts, were
her true landscape; but in her excitement and recognition
there was something of the exhilaration of Charles Doughty,
or of any of that band of her distinguished countrymen who
were drawn, as she now was, by the infinite mystery of
deserts and their clean, clear air. The pleasure was to make
its way into all she wrote; as a reviewer soon noted, Freya
had joined 'the odd handful who remained not to teach, not
to evangelize, not even, broadly speaking, to change, elevate,
govern or save but to understand, to interpret, to share the
life of the desert'.

After seven months, having spent the £200 she had saved
up, she left for Europe, 'with a feeling, dim but insistent,
that the whole of my future must be rearranged'. What she
needed now was a plan, perhaps a subject to research that
would return her to the East. Books of travel or history had
not really occurred to her, for she did not yet see herself as a
writer. A future among the missionaries was also dismissed,
since she had discovered that she hated philanthropy and
that her sense of curiosity made her a better student than a
teacher. If she regretted anything, it was the slowness with
which she was forming her own life, which came, she concluded, not from 'timidity, for I was morally brave by
nature, and physically by will' but from too strong a regard
for affection and a reluctance to waste any that came her

39

way. On a visit to London she spent her days in the British Museum, reading. The Jebel Druse was abandoned when she learnt that some fifty travellers had written about it already. 'I wonder', she noted gloomily, 'if there is anything left not written about? The only thing that is not overdone is *thinking*.'

In 1927, the Prime Minister of Iraq, Ja'far Pasha, having been approached by mutual friends, had invited Freya to visit Baghdad. Since then he had been appointed to London as ambassador, but her hopes of a visit remained, not least because she at last had a subject in mind: a history of the fortresses of the Assassins and their castles between Aleppo and the Persian border.

The Baghdad that Freya came to in the autumn of 1929 had been ruled over by King Faisal since 1921, when Iraq had been granted a monarchy by the British, but it was still firmly in British hands, run by British advisers and policed by British forces. The route out from Europe was by fast ship to Bombay, then by a slower one up the Persian Gulf to the port of Basra. For the last stage there was a train. Southern Mesopotamia, as the area had been known, lay between the rivers Tigris and the Euphrates; it was bare, barren and stony, prey to violent sandstorms. As the train neared Baghdad those watching from the windows could see great mounds of bare earth, all that remained of Babylon. (Other travellers preferred to come more of the way overland, boarding the Nairn brothers' articulated coach in Damascus, and drinking their whisky and soda through a straw as they bumped across the desert.)

The city itself had been little prepared for the grandeur of monarchy. In 1921 there had been no palaces or large buildings, only three bridges, made of boats, and only one street, unpaved and unpassable in rain. When Freya arrived, planning to spend some months preparing for an expedition into Persia, many of the brick houses were still unstable, lighting and sanitation were extremely primitive and a small fleet of horse-drawn carriages continued to be the main form of public transport. In the south of the country there were large numbers of Indians; in the north, many spoke only Turkish; in the north-east were the Kurds and the Yezidis, the 'devil-worshippers'. Nearly a third of the inhabitants of Baghdad were Jews. In the summer, the heat was intense, rarely falling below 110° in the shade; there were dust storms, severely trying to temper and nerves.

This was just the sort of place, with its mixed and exotic history and the desert stretching for miles beyond, that most appealed to Freya. What was more, it had a British past, a state of affairs she usually welcomed, with her firm approval of much of the legacy of Empire. There had been Englishmen in Baghdad for generations; a Residency had been established there in 1783 by the East India Company, after which had come a succession of well-intentioned representatives, like the scholarly Claudius James Rich, archaeologist of Babylon, and Henry Creswicke Rawlinson, who found the key to the cuneiform language by comparing the old Persian Elamite and the Babylonian inscriptions dedicated to Darius on the rock of Behistun, and who kept as pets a leopard, a lion cub and a mongoose. In 1929, when Freya arrived, Gertrude Bell, 'Um el-Muimin', mother of the faithful,

Oriental Secretary and Director of Antiquities, and translator
of Hafiz, had been dead just two years.

To the English community, centred round the handsome
colonial High Commission overlooking the river, with its fine
flowering verbena and wrought-iron gates and balconies,
Freya was a disconcerting arrival. She was thirty-six, small,
somewhat dumpy, very precise and sometimes steely in
manner and determinedly eccentric. She wore Arab dress for
dinner parties and a bandeau swathed across one side of her
face, where the scalp had been torn away. While they clustered at the Club, she sought lodgings with a shoemaker's
family, from financial necessity, since she had a very ordinary
liking for comfort. She furnished her room with a camp-bed,
and bought four ornamental candlesticks in the bazaar; she
was lent curtains and a sofa. From here she made sorties, by
rowing boat across the Tigris, to soirées where she observed
the local life, and the British in Baghdad.

She had not expected, she wrote home, to find them so
'hen-like' nor so full of 'froth and foam', though it was the
men, and not their wives, who were the more disapproving
of her. What had been necessary independence in Europe
was seen as wilful provocation in a city where rules of
behaviour were laid down in the clubhouse and the bar-
racks. When she proposed to spend a night at the camp of a
Bedouin sheik in the desert they were appalled and told her
that one could not be friends with both natives and the
British. She went just the same, after writing to the civil
servant who had reprimanded her that 'a dog is allowed
one bite before being suppressed; and I really haven't yet
had my bite'. Under a heavy black veil, she visited the

Kadhimaim mosque, so holy that no Christian was allowed inside and knowing that her visit was calculated to enrage all who learnt of it. She journeyed, on her own, north to Mosul, or with the Bedouin, into the desert. She attached herself to a harem for a few days near Damascus, where she came to feel ashamed of her unveiled condition, and soon objected to its 'deadly boredom' and gossip that reminded her forcefully of Dronero.

What she was doing, all this time, was beginning to develop her own style of observing and reporting. It was lively, detailed, revealing and often very personal, and it had not been much used among travellers of her kind before. To her mother, main recipient in these early years of the letters that were to be the backbone of future books, she described a visit to the Queen. 'It was after dinner because of Ramadan, and I wore my Asolo dress. We went up by a police sentry through miles of what might have been hospital corridors with very inferior coir matting spread along, and, instead of the Nubian slaves, little girls in high heels and knitted jumpers and an apron tied over them, who took our coats off. Then we went into a big room, rather bare walls, and crimson furniture – quite dignified in its bareness, and the little figure of the Queen, with an ermine wrap and gilt shoes, standing up very straight, and with a charming smile, in front of her crimson throne . . . A white fluffy cat sat under the throne and the white ermine. The Queen's face was ugly and charming – a huge mouth and henna'd hair which she has bobbed, but the only things noticeable are the vivid eyes so brimming with life that it seems a miracle she could say nothing.'

Privately, to friends in England, Freya was a little scornful of Gertrude Bell, whose ghost she complained resided over the city and who seemed to her overrated, for she had travelled with three baggage mules, two tents and three servants, had never had enough adventures, or stayed anywhere long enough to get to the heart of things.

In her notebook, elaborating on a philosophy for herself that she had touched on before and would return to constantly all her life, she wrote: 'So far as my personal object in life goes, I should wish to attain two things: first the confidence of more time, not to be confused within the narrow limits of one life: secondly, the sense of death as a new and wonderful adventure. If these two can attain a real sense of certainty, my own inner life will have succeeded – and I hope to succeed. It will mean the absolute liberation from fear, which is a form of slavery ... To risk one's life seems to me the only way in which one can attain to a real (as distinct from a merely theoretic) sense of immortality unless one happens to be among lucky people in whom faith is born perfect.'

Some of the bravado she kept up in public was genuine: Freya felt considerable and understandable contempt for the unthinking orthodoxy, cliquishness and racial superiority she encountered among many of the British families in Baghdad. (Through the columns of the *Baghdad Times*, she was later to poke fun at the rules governing the behaviour of those she referred to as the 'Ladies of Iraq'.) But some of it was show. In private, Freya was often low, hesitant and increasingly unhappy about her appearance and her solitariness. As she wrote to her mother, 'I am so very depressed this evening – feeling so old, and as if my whole life were wasted and it were now too late to do anything with it . . . and as if what I *do* do were not worth doing: no one seems to think it is, but just wonder at me and are sorry for me if they are nice, and disapprove if they are not. To be just middle-aged with no particular charm or beauty and no position is a dreary business . . . no one any longer makes love to me except when they are drunk.' Letters, her correspondence with friends in England, had become important to her; when post failed to come, she fretted.

To make things harder, Freya seems at this point to have fallen in love. Among the new friends she was making in Baghdad – and despite those who carped, there were now people, most of them men, who had come to admire her energy, her individuality and her considerable charm and who were to remain lifelong and devoted friends – was the man who had replaced Gertrude Bell as political adviser, Captain Vyvyan Holt, an exceptional Arabist, traveller and lover of the desert. It was not until 1942, summing up her life in a long unpublished letter to Sir Sydney Cockerell during a pause from the war on Cyprus, that she described to anyone what had happened. The incident, she wrote, had been a 'strange, unwanted falling in love, unprovoked and unexpected, inspired by the most conventional, unsuitable person who, for his part, hovered on the edge, but never fell in, and yet held me with no active effort of his own so that for seven years I never felt quite free . . . I regret walking so long down a one-way lane with only a blank wall at the end . . . The poverty of his affection saved me, and I kept my own way, but it was only with stress and trouble.'

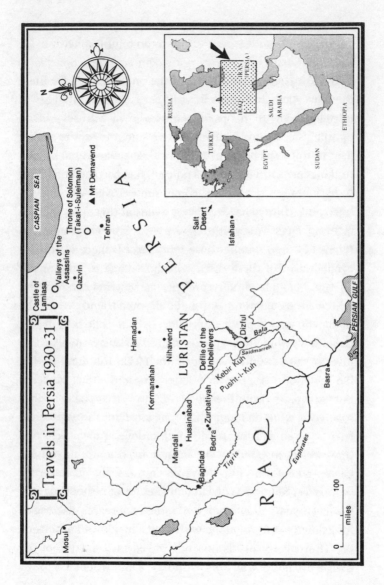

Travels in Persia 1930-31

It was through Holt, however, that Freya first began to learn Persian, and it was on his prompting that came the first true journey.

The Assassins were a Persian sect, a branch of the Shi'a Moslems, exploited by an unscrupulous Persian family who introduced them to rituals of initiation. Their first grand master was Hasan-i-Sabbah, who joined the sect in 1071, used murder and drugs as political tools, and became known to the West through the chronicles of the Crusaders. With some followers, Hasan seized a number of Syrian strong-holds and ruled over them as a semi-independent fief. His central fortress was at Alamut, in the unpassable mountain ridges of the Caspian, where he urged his men to practise the liberal arts while governing by assassination. In 1256 the Mongol armies came east; one by one they took the Assassin castles. (This, at least, was the contemporary thinking on the Assassins: a view since discredited by scholars.)

The idea that had come to Freya, sitting in the British Museum in London, was to travel across the area, fix the position of the fortresses, 'disentangle the absolute wrongness' of the map, and 'make for Alamut and Tehran across the jungle country – a lovely blank on the map so far'. Between April 1930 and October 1931 she made two main journeys into Persia, the first being interrupted by a characteristic piece of buccaneering on her part. At a Baghdad dinner party, someone had told her of a Lur boy who professed to have seen twenty cases of ornaments, daggers, coins and idols hidden in a cave in the limestone hills of Kebir Kuh in Luristan. Hoping for a glimpse of the treasure of Nihavend, Freya set up a short, and in the event

highly confused, side trip through unmapped country,
ending with a couple of hours when she shook off her at-
tentive police escort and scrambled, fruitlessly, about the
hills in search of the promised cave. It came to nothing, but
it was just the sort of outing she most enjoyed.

To practise Persian, Freya installed herself in the Hôtel de
France in Hamadan, and took lessons from a young man
dressed like a clown, with a henna'd beard, frock coat and
peaked cap. Every few days, she made short trips into the
mountains. After the desert and the dusty plains of Iraq,
Persia was enchantingly lush, a 'wonderful, wild, waste
country . . . tumbled seas of mountains, with pale green
valleys, very shallow, and blue and red ridges'. She travelled
always alone, and always, as the first European woman in
these parts a figure of intense curiosity and speculation, by
bus or by horse, and often on foot, with a guide, climbing
sometimes very high in search of clues to the lost Assassins.
In one valley a man told her of an ancient garden, 11,000
feet up, hidden by snow for several months each year. 'I got
so excited I felt my fingers trembling.'

In 1931 came the real expedition. One August morning,
with almost no money, having spent most of what she had
on emerald beads, she set out from Hamadan. 'This is a
great moment, when you see, however distant, the goal of
your wandering . . . It matters not how many ranges, rivers
or parching dusty ways may lie between you: it is yours
now forever.' As she journeyed, Freya gave names to the
mountain ranges and villages she passed through. She was
gone about four weeks. She found a missing castle, covering
the slanting top of a hill, surrounded by cliffs, with a secret

passage constructed down to the river, some 800 feet below. She reached it in her stockings, her shoes proving too slippery, and was gratified to hear a later expedition describe her route as 'unscaleable'.

Malaria, dengue fever, chronic dysentery, heart strain, measles – ill health has shadowed every adventure. 'It is now fourteen years that I have never once done anything without the feeling of fatigue, and I have only started on one of my expeditions without wondering if I was strong enough to face it', was how she once rebuked her seventy-six-year old mother, who was complaining about the disadvantages of age. High in the mountains, far from assistance, with the red pinnacles of the Alamut gorge in sight, she collapsed with dysentery. Then came malaria. Her watch stopped; she knew neither date nor time. For a week she thought she would die; but a diet of white of egg and sour milk, the kindness of the family with whom she lodged and above all her own indomitable disposition, pulled her through. She recorded the episode, the contemplation of death, the fear, the loneliness, dispassionately, sounding very human, but without complaint. It was her father's death, in Canada, that she had news of when she reached the diplomatic enclosure in Tehran.

The British in Baghdad were impressed. On her return there in the autumn of 1931, Freya found herself seated opposite an archdeacon at the Residency, a quite new and marked form of social approval. A perceptive editor of the *Baghdad Times*, Duncan Cameron, recognizing the potential in her increasingly assured tone and not unmalicious wit, offered her a job writing for the paper at a much-needed

£20 a month. Though Freya was not someone to enjoy the rigours of daily office life, she knew instinctively how to handle it. On her first day, no one rose as she entered the office. 'I made a little speech in the clerk's room explaining that office women are to be thought of as queens, and men stand up when they come in, and stand up they did, for the whole of the year that followed.'

In Persia, Freya had mapped a number of villages, identified two Assassin castles, gathered material for the first of her travel books, and made a first tentative try at archaeology, employing villagers to help her unearth some graves in Luristan to see whether men and horses were buried together. She had also discovered an intense pleasure in solitude and, more prosaically, had found she possessed a useful knack for falling instantly asleep, wherever she lay down. And she had created a style for her travels, lordly, distinctive, leisurely, fearless. But what made it most particularly her own was an often rather touching combination of self-humour and femininity. In a remote and utterly impoverished village, having conscientiously massaged her face with cold cream before retiring to bed, she offered some to the young village girls, who clustered always round her tent, thinking anxiously of their complexions.

'As I have the onus of making a precedent for any British lady who may ever come this way,' she wrote in one of her daily letters to her mother, 'I am trying to make her as comfortable as I can. I get my bed and net (so as to get some sort of privacy) put up in the open ... then get hot water provided: then turn everyone out of the harem and have a good wash.'

CHAPTER FOUR

Friends and Travellers

In the early summer of 1933, Freya arrived back in
London. She was forty. She had been in the East for more
than two years and was now emerging as a rather considerable figure, well versed in Arab matters and with a small,
but respectable, expedition behind her. The War Office had
approved her map of the Assassins' Valleys. The *Cornhill
Magazine* had already published a number of her articles on
the Druses and on a trip to Canada, when she had visited
her father's farm in British Columbia. With Jock Murray,
great-great-grandson of Byron's publisher, a 'slender young
man in tweeds', soon to become a devoted friend, she now
signed a contract for *The Valleys of the Assassins*. From their
first conversations, he was impressed by how meticulous
she was over corrections, how quick to see what needed
doing, able to re-paragraph and re-punctuate without hesita-
tion. There were rarely arguments; if she believed an
observation wrong, she said so, and made no changes.

After so much labour, and such personal uncertainty, the
public recognition must have been very pleasing. The Royal
Geographical Society presented her with its Back Grant, a

tribute to her travels in Luristan; the BBC asked her to
speak on the wireless; she lectured to the Royal Central
Asian Society and became the first woman to receive the
Burton medal of the Royal Asiatic Society. 'I always travel
alone and I am not frightened,' she told the distinguished
audience gathered for the occasion. 'I used to walk on ahead
of my miserable guide, because even a bandit would stop
and ask questions before shooting when he saw a European
woman strolling on alone, hatless.' It was all a long way
from the scorn of the Baghdad ladies. And then there was
the round of social engagements, tea with Sir Percy Cox,
first High Commissioner in Baghdad, to the House of
Commons with Lady Iveagh, and many new friends. 'I am
in such a vortex – parties all day long.'

One of these new friends was Lord David Cecil. He remembers with precision the first moment he became aware
of her. They were staying at Petworth. Their hosts, Lord
and Lady Leconfield, were extremely orderly, and had filled
the house with printed notices telling the guests where they
could and could not go. In the drawing room stood a table
covered with Dresden china; among the porcelain figures
was a notice: 'Do not handle the china'. As they rose to file
into dinner, Lord Cecil perceived a lady standing behind
him, smiling. She leant down, and picked up a piece of
Dresden. 'You see,' she said to him, enunciating very clearly,
in her formal, rather staccato voice, her eyes shining, 'I'm
handling the china.' It was Freya; they were friends from
that moment.

Another was Sir Sydney Cockerell, friend of Ruskin and
William Morris, director of the Fitzwilliam Museum in

Cambridge. After they met he wrote in his diary that he had been introduced to 'a nice Miss Stark, who has travelled alone in Persia and is going out again'. Cockerell was a great admirer of female charm, courage and worldly success; Freya possessed the first two, in quantity; she was unmistakably heading towards the third. By her next journey, she had become 'marvellous little Freya Stark, who is off once again . . .' Until his death in 1962, at the age of ninety-four, they were fond friends. He was the recipient of many hundreds of letters from her, including the long autobiographical letter from Cyprus, and it was he who instigated *Traveller's Prelude*, the first volume of her autobiography. They met at his house in Kew, for tea, whenever she was in London. 'You talk of such pleasant, quiet, happy, civilized things,' she told him; in his diary, he referred to these occasions as 'rapturous encounters'. Freya could take criticism from him in a way she could from very few others.

What people were now beginning to remark was that Freya was something rather unique in the world of explorers. It was not that where she travelled was very arduous or exotic, or that she was managing to move where no white traveller had gone before. Rather, there was something about her vision of things that singled her out, a certain quality to her observations, so that she appeared to relate landscape, people and their history, and make them all accountable for each other in some way peculiarly her own. She not only noted things that others had not perhaps thought important to record, but she wrote them down in such a way that they meant something to people who read them. The image she presented of Arabia, colourful, dignified, touched a chord in British minds, reared to regard the deserts and mountains of the Near East as settings of nobility and romance. History permeated her landscapes; and history, for Freya, meant not just wars and events but morality, that special quality that tied her to the Victorians.

'Her great role', says John Hemming, secretary of the Royal Geographical Society, 'was as a communicator. At a moment of doldrums for travellers and travel writing, people read and liked what she wrote.' There was another important point: she was a woman, and when she travelled, she went alone, with no money and no support.

Recognition in London as explorer and writer could do nothing for her appearance, however, which she continued to lament. 'Even now I cannot help thinking how much more fun to myself and others I might have procured, but for the absence of a few pigments, a millimetre here or there, a tiny tilt of chin or eyebrow, which those who possess them often scarcely know how to manipulate, and which I felt I might have animated to very great advantage.' But it could help with clothes. Between 1929 and 1934 she made, she recorded, £272 by writing; £155 was spent on dress. Clothes had always been important to her. (When W. P. Ker died, Viva Jeyes gave her a silk dress. 'There are few sorrows,' she remarked with a sort of sad satisfaction, 'through which a new dress or hat will not send a little gleam of pleasure however furtive.') Few years were now to go by without a new frock from Grès in Paris, a tailored Michael suit, a dashing little hat. It was not exactly vanity; more a delight in finery, a love of fabric and colour and plumage, compensation, perhaps, for the appearance she otherwise felt so dull.

It was probably at tea with Cockerell in November 1934 that Freya met the archaeologist Gertrude Caton Thompson for the first time. 'There were great talks', Cockerell recorded in his diary. Both women were evidently much interested in the south-west corner of Arabia and Freya at least was plotting a new trip, to the Yemen, 'practically *full* of things to discover', as she noted with pleasure.

The intense delight in departure, that moment of 'beckoning', never dulled for Freya; time after time, as the ship sets sail, the train draws away, a new note enters her writing. It is one of vigour, exultation, hopefulness. Her looks may have failed her, people may not have yielded all they seemed to promise, but here at least, her tone seems to suggest, in travel and new places and the remote rugged landscapes of Arabia, there will be no deceptions.

By the middle of January 1935, Freya was on a steamer travelling up the coast of South Arabia. She had paused briefly in Aden, where she had been befriended by a buccaneering figure very much in her own style, Anton Besse, a French merchant of silks and spices, friend of Rimbaud, lord of the Red Sea traffic and later founder of St Anthony's College in Oxford. Her goal was Shabwa in the Hadhramaut, alleged Himyaritic capital and centre of the incense trade, seven days' hard ride without water, never before visited by Europeans.

Her journey would not have been possible before. Until the previous year the Hadhramaut had been at war, split between two reigning dynasties, the Qu'aiti, who presided over the seaboard and the West, and the Kathiri, who held the inland eastern half. Neither had an organized government,

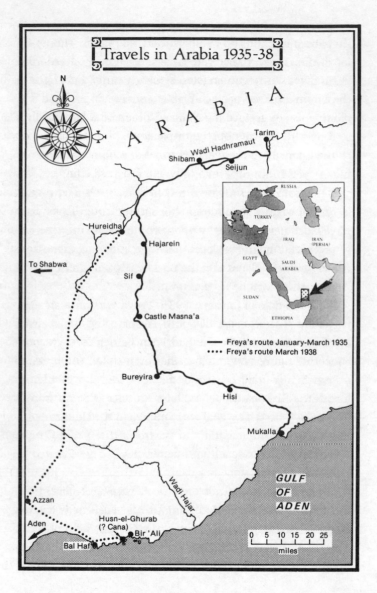

Travels in Arabia 1935-38

ARABIA

Tarim
Wadi Hadhramaut
Shibam
Seijun

Hureidha
Hajarein

To Shabwa
Sif

Castle Masna'a

Bureyira
Hisi

Mukalla

——— Freya's route January-March 1935
••••• Freya's route March 1938

GULF OF ADEN

Azzan
Aden
Husn-el-Ghurab
(? Cana)
Bir 'Ali
Bal Haf

Wadi Hajar

0 5 10 15 20 25
miles

RUSSIA
TURKEY
EGYPT
IRAQ
IRAN (PERSIA)
SAUDI ARABIA
SUDAN
ETHIOPIA

their Sultans ruling more or less personally with local tribesmen. Late in 1934, Harold Ingrams, Political Officer in the Aden Protectorate (which covered 112 square miles and was in treaty relations with twenty tribal states, to whom it offered protection in exchange for goodwill and the promise of no meddling in the colony of Aden), had ridden out with his wife Doreen on a camel, on a mission to pacify and conciliate the warring tribes.

On 21 January 1935, with cameras, compass, range-finder, clinometer and aneroid, riding on a donkey and accompanied by guides, Freya set out from the sea town of Mukalla, where she had been staying with the Sultan. Hadhramaut means 'death is present'. She rode through desert not of sand but of stones, stretching mile after mile across a plateau, with emptiness extending to the horizon. In the villages, built on the edge of wadis, where she was guest of the local ruler, she visited the harems, listened, observed and talked, in her Arabic that was rapidly becoming fluent and colloquial. Everywhere, she took photographs of landscapes, mountains, wadis, villages and people, lining them up firmly before the camera when they drew back; the results were remarkable, recording people and places never seen before, frozen at one of the last moments when travel was still exploration.

In Masna'a, a medieval castle town, six days' ride into the desert, as ever prey to a jinx on her health, she caught measles and was kept confined for days, having been told by local women that she must not smell any kind of scent, for it would rush to the head, which because of the dryness of the air, would swell and burst. When she recovered, she was lent a horse and rode on to Seijun, another medieval town surrounded by cliffs, where the women wore long blue gowns and 'Welsh high hats' and a family of rich Java merchants gave her a room looking out over palm trees.

Shibam, known to later travellers as the 'skyscraper town of the desert' for its tapering, many-storied mud-and-brick houses which, as the population multiplied, grew upwards, not being able to move outwards because of the encircling city wall, was to have been Freya's casting-off point for Shabwa. When she got there she again fell ill. This time it was serious. Measles, then dysentery and the strain of the journey seem to have affected her heart. As in Luristan, she thought she was about to die. What she minded more than anything was that a German traveller had now appeared in Shibam and that he too was on his way to Shabwa. 'I know it is vulgar to want to *be the first*, but yet it is so bitter when one has come so far,' she wrote to a friend in London. From her bed, when not consoling herself with Virgil, she did her best to stir up anti-German feeling among the Bedouin.

On 15 March, four bombers from the RAF, on a practice flight of the area, bore her off on a stretcher to Aden hospital from where she wrote miserably to her mother: 'I suppose I have dished women's chance of going alone for at least half a generation . . .'

However acute the disappointment, her travels were enough to make a book. *The Southern Gates of Arabia*, published a year later, received warm reviews. Cockerell called it 'a masterpiece', and the Royal Scottish Geographical Society chose this moment to present her with their Mungo Park medal.

It was now that Freya and Gertrude Caton Thompson, herself winner of several impressive awards, met to discuss the possibility of digging together in the Hadhramaut, in order to establish whether there had been some cultural contact between Arabia and Africa during the Roman period. They had found a third companion, Elinor Gardner, a geologist, and backing, from the Royal Geographical Society and from Lord Wakefield, financial godfather to many such adventures, who presented Freya with a cheque for £1,500.

The party met in Port Said, Freya joining them after a separate trip to the holy Shi'a cities of Njef and Kerbala, which left her remarking sadly on the struggle for freedom she had witnessed everywhere, and concluding that both French and British efforts failed, 'the former by adulterating their teaching by the pursuit of power, the latter by too often forgetting that they are there to teach'.

They travelled to Aden by P. & O., in great heat; the Red Sea was rough. In the hold were seventy-one packages and bales of provisions, an 'immense but rather dreary food list' as Freya commented somewhat archly, adding that a dietitian had observed it was sufficient for the 'very poor in a hot climate: for those who have nothing to do'. Otherwise, her tone was meek. 'I am just nothing,' she wrote to a friend, 'but expect as much fun out of it as any.'

There was not much fun to be had. It is possible that the expedition was always fated, from the very first day when the two distinguished travellers, one an Arabist, the other an Egyptian and African expert, sat discussing their dreams over a cup of tea in Cockerell's drawing room. Neither Freya

nor Miss Caton Thompson was accustomed to doing anything but lead; neither, now, was willing to take second
place. (Miss Gardner, malleable, accommodating, desired no
other position.)

In Aden, the SS *Narkunda* was met by Stewart Perowne,
an ADC sent out by the Governor to collect some visiting oil
magnates, who sped the party to shore in the official launch.
He and Freya discussed Milton and Tennyson. She found
him 'gay, slim, well dressed, enthusiastic, with a sparkle
that matched the sunlight in the bay'. Soon the three ladies,
quickly dubbed the 'three foolish virgins' by the more
malicious old Aden hands, were ensconced on the Ingrams'
roof at Mukalla, falling asleep in night temperatures that
never fell below 85°, badly bitten by sandflies, and overcome
by the stench of the local delicacy, rotting shark. Freya,
muttering crossly that she seemed to have become a 'glori-
fied courier', remarked that her two companions wandered
with their eyes to the ground while she was 'inclined to
gossip with all the neighbourhood which slowly gathers
and drifts along with us, offering bits of hopeful rubbish'.
Gertrude Caton Thompson, used to the Egyptians, dismissed
all those who thronged around with disdain; for Freya, a
basic rule of travelling was that one should sit around and
be pleasant.

The excavation headquarters were at Hureidha, a village
lying on the corner of the Wadi Hadhramaut. It was surrounded by sand dunes, stony dry water-courses and fields
of wheat and millet, guarded by mud forts. Lodgings for
them and their servant Qasmin were found in a small brown
house on a hillside above the village, sheltered by the cliff,

with a view over a castle. The dig began; a temple was uncovered, then some graves. The following year, when Doreen Ingrams visited Hureidha, the small boys were fascinated by her shoes, but disappointed, for, they told her, Freya's had 'much higher heels. In the name of God most high and the religion He glorifies, you couldn't walk in them they were so high.'

By the end of November, Elinor's throat was giving trouble, Gertrude was pining for London and Freya was saying that she had always known that she would end up as nurse. 'There are not many born travellers, though they think they are . . . I hate archaeology if it means that one's whole soul has to turn into statistics and eliminate human beings . . . You may not believe it, but with Gertrude our *whole* conversation is either ancient flints or tinned food: there seems no half-way house.'

With more than a passing touch of reflective malice, Freya sat down one day and sketched out the qualities of the true traveller. 'Last night,' she wrote to her mother, 'I made a list (for myself) of the seven cardinal virtues for a traveller:

1. To admit standards that are not one's own standards and discriminate the values that are not one's own values.
2. To know how to use stupid men and inadequate tools with equanimity.
3. To be able to dissociate oneself from one's bodily sensations.
4. To be able to take rest and nourishment as and when they come.

5. To love not only nature but human nature also.
6. To have an unpreoccupied, observant and un-censorious mind – in other words to be unselfish.
7. To be as calmly good tempered at the end of the day as at the beginning.

'And,' she could not resist adding, 'I should like to see Gertrude trying to conform to *one* of them.'

It would have been funny had it not been so tense. They must have been a curious party, the three excessively English ladies: Gertrude off digging whenever she could, Elinor sifting through her rocks, while Freya wandered or sat writing, all against a gentle but incessant bickering, while fevers raged and the heat rose into the hundreds. The problem, for Freya, lay only with Gertrude, who minded very much who was in charge, and while she would not tolerate Freya interfering with her flints, spent much time meddling with what Freya called 'human relations'. 'I think', noted Freya, 'I shall emerge from this winter an anti-feminist, because really women might be a little nicer to each other: they practise none of the graces of life . . .' The words are revealing. By the end of the thirties, Freya had very strong views as a traveller, she did find most women irritating and unquestionably preferred men, and, even so, only the deference which her upbringing had instilled in her to regard men with respect ever made them tolerable as travelling companions. Gertrude and Elinor were doomed.

At the beginning of March the party split up. Gertrude and Elinor set off thankfully back towards Cairo, while Freya decided on a last solitary exploration of South

Arabia, a month's ride along an unvisited incense route to the coast through the tribal borderlands of the west, to try to establish the whereabouts of the Himyaritic harbour of Cana, emporium of the incense trade. She left, perched high on a camel, under her sunshade. It was a gruelling 120-mile ride. Yet again she was not well, afflicted with what turned out to be dengue fever. At Azzan, still some twenty miles from her destination, she was warned against journeying alone through dangerous countryside, hostile to infidels. She made it to the coast by joining a well-armed caravan of twenty-seven camels, carrying tobacco, with a bodyguard of twelve soldiers and four relations of the Sultan of Azzan. She brought with her a lizard, named Himyar after his mountain home, clasped to her under a quilt.

At Balhaf, on the coast, a dismal, volcanic spot, the caravan unloaded the tobacco onto a boat. Freya was still some eight hours' ride from her real objective, the town of Husn-el-Ghurab. She travelled on, having been promised a boat to carry her back to Balhaf. At Husn-el-Ghurab she found buildings, fortifications and cisterns, all consistent with its claims to be Cana, and noted 'crocodile black snouts of lava, half submerged, push through ... everywhere. Beyond, in a sea misty with sunlight, are the islands as the Peripeus describes them ...' While she was wandering in the town, the inhabitants gathered and began to threaten; there was talk of shooting; the boat had not turned up. Freya climbed back onto her camel and rode to Balhaf through the night. Before she left, while waiting to discuss her future with a deputation of village leaders, came a characteristic bit of bravado: 'I was beyond anything else thirsty. "Are they sending the boat and the water?" I asked.

' "They are sending the water, but no boat." Their methods of warfare, I could not help feeling, compared favourably with those of Europe.

'It was time to attend to the bewildered envoys. Diplomatically speaking, we had the situation in hand. "Welcome and ease." I said. "When are you coming to shoot us?" '

Later, Freya described her expedition in *The Times*, and in a lecture to the Royal Geographical Society. Though others before her had suggested Husn-el-Ghurab for Cana, no one had produced such detailed and careful descriptions of the surrounding countryside. 'The average Englishman', wrote Sir Kinahan Cornwallis, the distinguished Arabist and diplomat, in a foreword to *A Winter in Arabia*, Freya's book on the Hadhramaut, 'is not blessed with an exaggerated sense of imagination in his dealings with other races, but it is to be hoped that all who read Miss Stark's pages will learn the difference between the right way and the wrong, and profit thereby.'

The months of unhappy partnership, under Freya's pen, made their way into the book. She started with a ferocious attack on Gertrude Caton Thompson, but her asperity was toned down by Cockerell (to no more than a few acid asides about an unnamed archaeologist, and a smug comment that whenever Freya spoke of her companions to the women of Hureidha, they spat), though not before some ruthless fighting with Jock Murray, to whom she protested bitterly that cutting would destroy all point to her words.

Freya's father, Robert Stark, painted by his wife, Flora

Freya with her younger sister, Vera, in England, 1898

Freya in Asolo, 1902

View from Casa Freya in Asolo, taken by Herbert Young in 1897

Freya on her desert travels in the 1930s

Opposite: *From top left to bottom right*
Sir Sydney Cockerell;   W. P. Ker;
Freya with Bernard Berenson at Asolo, 1955;
Field Marshall Archibald Wavell;   Jock Murray

The house Freya shared in Hureidha with Gertrude Caton Thompson and
Elinor Gardner in the winter of 1937–8
Alwiyeh, Freya's house in Baghdad during 1941–2
Both photographs were taken by Freya herself

Freya with Stewart Perowne

Freya at the revolving desk in her study at Asolo

Freya at 91 when she was presented with the keys of Asolo in May 1984

Montoria, near Asolo, the house Freya built in 1963

Miss Caton Thompson waited over forty years before taking her revenge. In 1983 she brought out her autobiography, *Mixed Memoirs*; the Freya who emerges from Chapter 23, clearly named and identified, is inefficient, quarrelsome, imperious, unscrupulous and, noted the ninety-year-old author with a kind of tart relish, had been called a 'bloody bitch' by the pilot who had come fruitlessly in search of her when she was ill. 'Which,' she concluded sombrely, 'I thought moderate in the circumstances.'

Freya returned to a Europe on the brink of the Munich crisis, bringing with her Himyar, who had developed an expensive taste for violets, and forever disillusioned with archaeology: 'It means seeing nothing but the dead,' she complained in a letter to Cockerell, 'and the living world is too beautiful and vivid for that.' She sat writing in Asolo, waiting for a coded telegram from Lady Iveagh in London. When it came all it said was 'Olga dying'. 'Olga' meant peace. Freya packed, caught the Orient Express from Venice and was in Paris ordering a final hat when she saw Hitler's ultimatum to Czechoslovakia printed, like a funeral announcement, in thick black letters.

There was just time for one more journey. Early in 1939 she travelled for a last look at the Crusader castles. On the way up to Krak des Chevaliers a guide tried to plunder her baggage. Instead of cowering, Freya rounded on him, rallied the others, and having subdued him continued to berate him all the way down the mountain; when he sought to kiss her hand, she pulled it away. The incident said much about how she saw herself as a traveller, intrepid, yet respectful of the dignity of those among whom she travelled, a woman alone, subduing bandits by superior moral strength. It was also the same spirit of courage that prompted her, when in her late seventies, to pursue a band of robbers from her remote house in the foothills of the Dolomites, firing a revolver over their heads. She later explained that she had had to shoot, otherwise no one would have believed her capable. A last series of short visits, then back 'to look again at Greece before the curtain fell'.

CHAPTER FIVE

The Brotherhood of Freedom

Freya began the war in London as a South Arabia expert for the Ministry of Information. She was given a salary of £600 a year and immediately spent some of it on what she considered the basic necessities for a prolonged war: a little bag for all 'one's toilet things to take with me to the basement . . . a winter suit . . . and French face powder which we may never see again for the next five years'. Within a couple of weeks came a request from Stewart Perowne, now Information Officer in Aden, to join him as his assistant. Pausing in Asolo to collect a trunk of tropical clothes and in Cairo where she noted approvingly that the women were wearing scented jasmine around their wrists for parties, she reached Aden in November.

Before the Suez Canal was built, Aden was a coaling station on the route to India. It had been a British colony for just over a century, Captain Stafford Bettesworth Haines having captured the rocky promontory in the name of Queen Victoria in January 1839, and turned it into a prosperous merchant city. At the outbreak of war a rich ship-owning family had donated a building to the British as a free war gift, and it was here that Freya came to work and live, up steep wooden stairs, with a terrace overlooking the harbour. Her two personal rooms were full of hefty Victorian furniture and hung with stately royal portraits. She woke, in a mahogany four-poster bed, to distant muezzin calls to prayer. There was a secretary called Dyllis and a translator called Ali Muhammad.

From her two earlier journeys in the Hadhramaut, Freya still had a number of friends in Aden. They did not give her quite the welcome she hoped for. Gertrude Caton Thompson, travelling back through the city at the end of their winter in Hureidha, had managed to add her own voice to an opinion gaining some ground that, though fascinating and full of charm, Freya as a traveller could be ruthless, too quick to use others and lazy in her gratitude.

Whatever reserve may have been felt locally was soon dispelled by the war. Stewart Perowne put her to writing a summary of the day's news which Ali would translate into Arabic so that it could be broadcast from a loudspeaker in the square after evening prayer. The news started out as truthful; as reports from Europe grew more worrying, 'we stressed the celestial city in the distance and pointed out with stronger emphasis the temporary nature of those swamps and thickets that lay in the immediate path'. It was the sort of thing Freya was best at.

Life in Aden was agreeable. Freya rose early, drove out by taxi beyond the peninsula, by windmills and saltpans, and rode around the dunes, skirting the gardens of a Sheikh Othman which smelt 'like all the spices of Arabia'. Sometimes she saw flamingoes. In the evenings, after work, she gave a glass of vermouth to anyone who turned up on her terrace, and they sat watching the lights of the ships in the bay. There were dinner parties in Government House with Sir Bernard Riley, bridge games at the Union Club and dances for the soldiers on their way out to India. Her relations with Stewart Perowne were very cordial; almost flirtatious. On her arrival she had found him 'long-necked and bald-headed like a young vulture, but with none of that pompous slowness which gives vultures their official look . . .' To Cockerell, she wrote that he treated her as if she were his wife, always expecting her to be there, but giving her no information to go on. 'I keep him in a state of mild but continuous exasperation. Do you think it's a sign of love or hate? It seems quite pleasant anyway.' To escape the constant work, she insisted on 'two walks a week in the hills to listen to silence'.

Towards the end of the year, Sir Kinahan Cornwallis, then in Political Intelligence, wrote to ask for information, particularly on the Yemen where the Italians and Germans were active. It was the sort of request that appealed to Freya. She despatched one of her most forthright and reasoned letters back, arguing that the British were doing wrong in not taking the Italians more seriously, and suggesting a 'riposte to every Italian step'. What she proposed to do, she said, was to smuggle a portable projector into the Yemen, with a number of very British films. 'The idea is to sit there, visit harems, rectify rumours and alter the atmosphere as much as one can from the standpoint of female insignificance, which has its compensations.'

Sana, the walled capital of Yemen, was like a medieval

European town. The narrow streets were lined with craftsmen, polishing gems and carving daggers; down them wound an endless procession of men leading donkeys and camels. Freya reached the city by lorry, 'like a new weapon of iron into the bronze age', with a cook, a servant and three other men, having taken six days up the torrent beds of the northern frontier. She found a state ruled over with 'religious fastness' by the Imam Jahya, so that toys showing the human form were confiscated. It was as well that she had thought to hide her projector. There were a number of Italians, who had cornered the medical field, and a small British community who possessed the only tennis court.

Obedient to local custom, Freya was fed by the palace kitchens for the first few days, given a guard of three soldiers and lodged in the Turkish suburb in a house among gardens. In the first week she taught the Imam's cook to make butter and translated a telegram from King George into Arabic. For the next two months, she visited harems, peering with the women through carved lattices at the busy life of the town below, and infiltrating her cinema into their rooms. Soon she was showing to a different harem every night. Never practical, she found setting up the performance, while stumbling over women and children, threading the film and setting up the screen, extremely nerve-racking. She had three military films with her, but found that *Ordinary Life in Edinburgh* went down best with the ladies of the court.

By March she felt that she had done as much damage to the Italian mission as she could, having obviously derived considerable enjoyment out of teasing them. 'This place', she wrote to Stewart, 'is now fairly convinced that Britain is *strong.*' She returned to Aden in time for the air raids, for Italy had now declared war. Soon a ship was sunk outside the bay; then a submarine was captured. As Freya knew Italian, she was invited to breakfast on the Admiral's flagship, to look at captured papers and to translate in the interrogation of survivors.

While on her way to join Stewart Perowne in Aden the previous autumn, Freya had spent a night at the British Embassy in Ankara. There she met 'an officer with many ribbons, active, not tall, with grizzled hair and a steadfastness as of friendly granite all about him; and in his general expression, a look of gaiety and youth'. It was General Wavell. By 1940 he was Commander-in-Chief in Cairo. Feeling in need of a break, Freya now set off for Egypt, where she bought herself a 'Molyneux creation' and went to call on Wavell. The moment had come, she argued, to encourage a raid on the hinterland of Genoa and to rally the anti-fascists. Wavell was a notoriously silent man. He said nothing. Even Freya was somewhat intimidated. Eventually he spoke: 'I have no troops to spare.' This was an improbable start to a friendship, but Wavell and Freya were to be close friends from this time on. Though she was unable to launch a battle, Freya got herself transferred to Cairo, at double her existing salary, and somewhat to Stewart Perowne's annoyance.

Early in September, Freya settled into a flat in Zamalek, on the edge of the Nile. From her terrace, she could watch the ibis and the barges on the river. She bought two carpets, a silver coffee-pot and a baby Austin, telling Stewart

Perowne that 'one has to live dangerously somehow in wartime' (Freya's driving was almost too dangerous to be a joke; people spoke of her, when at the wheel, accelerating down the troop-filled streets, as one of the 'chief menaces to the general safety of Egypt'). Cairo was very gay. There were dinners and dances at the British Embassy, set among wide lawns on the edge of the Nile, with buckets of roses and silver plates, and the soldiers all in their mess jackets. There might be breakfast with General 'Jumbo' Wilson, and talk about when to invade Italy; perhaps lunch at the Turf Club with Steven Runciman, a tea party on her terrace, then on to drinks at Shepheard's Hotel, with some of the soldiers back on leave from the front. Freya spent Christmas in Luxor with the ambassador, Sir Miles Lampson, and his wife, dancing with the pashas in the evening and galloping on donkeys across the desert in the day.

She was, however, also hard at work. When Freya reached Cairo, General Graziani was at the Western desert frontier, advancing with 300,000 men. There were some 80,000 Italians in Egypt, most of them inclined towards fascism. The intention behind Freya's appointment was to help find a way of keeping on the British side the Egyptians whom the fascist Italian colony were trying to undermine. To this work Freya brought a new idea of her own. Propaganda, she had decided, was a wrong word to focus on, since it implied a sinister twist of deceit. What was needed instead was persuasion, and that entailed commitment on the part of the person practising it; it had to be of advantage to both speaker and listener; and the local people themselves had to interpret and distribute the words. Encouraging would-be friends, not proselytizing enemies, was her goal.

Freya's chosen tool was something she had been thinking about ever since war broke out. This was a network of committees or cells, who would meet, and talk, in a pro-ally, pro-British spirit. The Brothers and Sisters of Freedom, as they were soon named, began by meeting on her terrace over coffee. Then they spread to other parts of Cairo. All kinds of people joined in, both Egyptian and foreign, and within a couple of months Freya had been invited to speak at the Azhar University, stronghold of Moslem learning.

Nominally, Freya was attached to the embassy. Much of her time, however, was spent in her baby Austin, visiting cells, first in Cairo, later, as the Brotherhood spread, in the villages. In Alexandria, where a cell was started by a rich contractor, Abd-al-Khalil Kinawi, it soon grew enormous, particularly among the workers from the dockyards.

During the autumn, Freya was joined by Pamela Hore-Ruthven, whose husband Pat was fighting in the desert, and Lulie Abul Huda, Oxford educated and daughter of a prominent Turkish-Egyptian family. Pamela Hore-Ruthven spoke no Arabic, but was tall, fair-haired, beautiful and had many friends; Lulie Abul Huda had both friends and perfect Arabic. They started out with a plump Coptic assistant and twenty camel drivers. Freya worked them hard. Considerably older than any of them, she seemed inexhaustible, sitting bolt upright in her tight European suits and extraordinary hats, talking for hour upon hour, listening, reasoning. 'She was never lackadaisical,' remembers Pamela Hore-Ruthven. 'She did hope to find others to do the donkey work – but if they didn't, she did it herself. She had this extraordinary faith in Britain winning the war. There was something in that short, tough body that never doubted about British Empire.'

Reactions to the Brotherhood in Cairo were mixed, with the older Turkish aristocracy regarding the 'whisperers' with some suspicion, as 'intelligence', while some of the British diplomats mocked it, or wondered whether it shouldn't concern itself exclusively with women, something Freya was adamantly opposed to. Among the military, however, there was little but admiration for Freya, whether for her tenacity and enterprise or her charm, and among the young soldiers in particular she was soon something of a mascot, in her improbable clothes, with her quick repartee, and a way of talking the young men found 'not exactly erudite, but wonderfully philosophical'. With those just back from the desert, she could be flirtatious, in an intellectual sort of way. She was both very wise and charmingly, absurdly innocent. They felt they grew up, listening to her talk.

By the end of 1941, the Brotherhood had 400 members; in the following years it spread up and down the Nile so that by January 1942 there were thought to be some 6,000 people pledged to fight the fifth column. Only by then Freya was long since gone, having carried her weapon of persuasion with her to Iraq.

In April 1941, four Iraqi colonels, known as the Golden Square and heavily influenced by the Germans, seized power in Baghdad. They were led by a politician called Rashid Ali

Gailani. They took over the post office and the radio station and entered the palace to arrest the British-supported regent, Emir Abdulillah, uncle of the young King Faisal the second, only to find him gone, having been spirited out of Baghdad, hidden under rugs at the back of a car, by the American minister Mr Knabenshue.

The British community was in a state of some flux, with a new ambassador, Sir Kinahan Cornwallis, distinguished Arabist and former British adviser, arriving. There were rumours, uncertainties, a pause, during which Cornwallis arranged for the landing of British troops at Basra. A second landing of troops triggered off the start of hostilities in the desert. The embassy was besieged.

Freya was one of the last to arrive in Baghdad before its gates closed. She had been travelling in Persia and had hastened south, driving up, she later explained to Cockerell, through 'about 5,000 students with banners, and dancing and patriotic yells. They engulfed the car and surged along on either side, giving it a kick or a spit now and then; I kept smiling . . .'

While one rescue party set off from Basra, and another from Transjordan, the embassy settled down to its siege. There were about 350 people, including the servants, but very few women, the wives and children having been flown out to India. It was the kind of situation Freya greatly enjoyed. While the gardeners went on watering the cypresses and the verbena, she recruited Seton Lloyd, former adviser to the Iraqi Department of Antiquities, to help her monitor the foreign news and prepare a daily bulletin for the embassy. Since all the other radios had been confiscated, they listened to one in a car, parked on the lawn. To this day Seton Lloyd can remember Freya's cross voice saying: 'We've *heard* all this,' as the dim voices from Jerusalem crackled and faded.

Freya's morale was superb. Spurning the dormitory set aside for the ladies she took her mattress up to the terrace and slept in a corner overlooking the Tigris from where she could watch the police launches chugging up and down the river and keep an eye on the crowds gathering in the upper town. Through Vyvyan Holt's good relations with the Ministry of Foreign Affairs, fresh food was brought in every day; Freya put in a request for face powder for the ladies, causing a policeman on the gate to remark how strange it was that English women could think about their faces when they were shortly to be massacred.

With these policemen she was at her most lordly. When a British reconnaissance plane came over they lifted their guns and fired. Freya, standing near, expressed immense disdain. 'You know best, madam,' one of the men said, and put down his rifle. In the evening, there were rationed drinks served on the lawn; at dawn Holt could be seen exercising his polo ponies in a corner of the compound. As the days went by, Newton, the butler, offered to whiten Freya's shoes. It was British frontier spirit at its best.

On 28 May guns could be heard from the north, where a column led by the Arab Legion was cutting off the rebels' retreat. Inside Baghdad, two battalions turned against Rashid Ali and the colonels fled to Persia. The siege was over.

It ended with characteristic British Empire dash. On 30

May a message from the town came to say that a deputation, led by the lord mayor, would like to see the ambassador. Through the wicket gate filed the mayor, followed by the chief of police and a very young commander-in-chief of the Iraqi troops. They were shown into the ambassador's study, where immediately the commander began to shout and gesticulate, and express his hope that the British would know how to respect the independence of Iraq. Cornwallis was well over six foot tall, a quiet man with a long, distinguished nose. He listened patiently. When silence finally settled on the gathering, he spoke, in perfect Arabic. 'I had the privilege of serving his Majesty King Faisal the first. With him, I assisted in creating the Iraqi nation. I do not intend to be lectured by young men who were in shorts at that time.'

Few in Baghdad believed that the British victory over the rebels was more than a set-back to German plans. The Vichy French in Syria were busy refuelling German planes and in Crete there had been a serious defeat of the Allied troops. Her transfer requested by Cornwallis, Freya now prepared to set up her Brotherhood in Iraq, though in a somewhat muted form, as Freya felt the country was not ready for anything as specific as Brotherhood cells.

In mid-October Freya found a house in Alwiyah, the Hampstead of Baghdad, modelled on British Indian army cantonment lines, with detached single-storey bungalows set among lawns and oleanders. Pamela Hore-Ruthven arrived to help her, and later, after she left, Peggy Drower, a fluent Arabist and the daughter of old Baghdad friends of Freya's. Once again, Freya set them a punishing routine.

Occasionally they felt like slaves, Freya having decided that office grind was not for her. There were meetings to set up, the news to be gathered and sifted, a bulletin to be written and copied. Most time-consuming were the 'Qabul', the 'At Homes', a regular feature of Baghdad life, to which ladies simply went along uninvited and ate cakes, and which Freya and Peggy Drower used as occasions for pro-British chat. One week, Freya noted that she had attended thirteen. After the Brotherhood took serious root, there were also trips to set up cells among the Marsh Arabs and the Kurds.

Against this background of continual occupation, Freya always found time for reflection. 'Very few people who think much seem really convinced of personal immortality,' she wrote to Cockerell. 'I myself . . . came to the simple faith that what had no beginning could have no end . . . When I was so near death once or twice the cold and bleak prospect frightened me: since then, however, a strange reassurance has come and I *think* I could no longer feel that fear: I know that in moments of great ecstasy even in this life you cease to be "personal" at all: your whole being is merged and loses itself as it were, even in such daily things as the loveliness of a sunset or a rose: if such is the loss of personality, and I believe it to be so, it does not seem to matter.' She was to repeat this, often, later.

As in Cairo, wartime life in Baghdad could be very pleasant. Though something of a backwater, the city was full of soldiers and provided a centre for British intelligence, which soon gathered to it many friends of Freya's, and many others who were to become friends. 'It is so nice', she remarked, 'to be mate and not skipper . . .' There was Adrian Bishop, in charge of the Special Operations Executive, Teddy Hodgkin, Aidan Philip and Stewart Perowne, now posted as information officer to Iraq. There was the embassy itself, with Vyvyan Holt as Oriental Secretary. In the early mornings horses were brought to the door of the little pink villa in Alwiyah and Freya rode out into the desert with Stewart Perowne, or her young paying guest, Nigel Clive. At weekends there were picnics by the river, with Seton and Ulrica Lloyd, who took their mongoose with them to swim. And there were always parties. Freya, never dull, was capable of great, enjoyable frivolity. Robin Maugham, visiting Baghdad, was taken to dine with her. 'I had imagined a rather gaunt, tough traveller,' he wrote in his autobiography, *Nomad*. 'I found a small, sprightly lady . . . with her head on one side like a bird, inquiring, with clear, piercing eyes beneath fine brows.'

This was a good time for Freya. She had a steady income, her health was good and she had been made temporary Attaché at the embassy. It was fun to have the Prime Minister, Nuri Pasha, to dinner and to discuss military strategy with Jumbo Wilson; reassuring to learn from the ambassador that what she was doing was important. Rightly, she could feel appreciated, able at last to exercise some influence on policy. (Even if she was also short of funds. She wanted £9,300 for her committees. Stewart Perowne, her superior, refused to authorize payment for anything he had not approved. Freya got her own back by putting down a new typewriter to 'telephones', arguing that 'they all seemed the same to me, the same sort of mechanical *idea*, and telephones was the only heading that had money left'.) Everywhere from Delhi to Washington she could count on influential friends. In her support of the 'young effendis', the new, educated, middle-class Arabs, the product of the 'internal combustion engine, the (mostly) American educator, and the British Government' now chafing for power, she saw herself as helping to mould a better post-war Middle East.

There was also truth in her conviction that the Brotherhood was important. If there were some in Baghdad who argued that it couldn't possibly reach the young intellectuals who really mattered, and others who said that Freya would do better to talk less herself and listen more to others, whose English was better than her Arabic, there were many more prepared to vouch that it played its part in keeping Iraq friendly, in persuading the Iraqis, and particularly the women, that English people were perfectly reasonable, that their ideology was acceptable, and that they were neither as aloof nor as foreign as they had seemed before.

In November 1942, Freya heard that her mother had died. To the sadness of her loss was added guilt, for she felt responsible for some of the difficulties of her mother's last years. In May 1940 she had sent her an urgent warning from Aden to leave Asolo, where she and Herbert Young were living in the house that had been left to Freya. They tried to get visas for Switzerland or America, but they were turned down. Freya, locally, was believed to be a British spy, and, though no one ever actually established the connection, two weeks after Italy declared war, Flora and Herbert Young were taken to the gaol in Treviso, where Flora, upright, very gracious in her high-necked blouses, found herself incarcerated with thieves and prostitutes. Later, Flora wrote a charming memoir of her imprisonment. Penal life in wartime Italy was as feudal as any outpost of Empire. Wardens and inmates alike did their best to cosset Flora. When one used bad language, the others made a loud noise to conceal the words. Marina Volpe, daughter of the finance minister, and an Asolo neighbour, brought her three pairs of white cotton gloves, having noticed that Flora's chamois ones needed washing.

After a few weeks, they were released and by September allowed back to Asolo, where Herbert Young, already frail, soon died. Flora, at seventy-eight as handsome as ever, greatly loved by the whole village, left for California, where she lived with friends. Her death made a terrible hole in Freya's life. For all the betrayals of childhood, the falling out over Guido and Vera, Freya had remained exceptionally close to her, writing to her at least once and often several times a week, a cosy intimate correspondence that had gone on for over forty years. The relationship had never been simple; there was too much ambiguity, too much history in it, to make it always pleasurable, but it answered a need in Freya that nothing else seemed able to. To friends in Baghdad, she seemed very wretched. 'I feel', she wrote sadly, 'as if no one in all the world belongs to me and it is rather like being in a room far too big for one.'

There was, however, much to cheer her up. That month *Letters from Syria*, a selection of pre-war letters edited by Cockerell, was published in London. It sold 4,000 copies before publication. And in June the Royal Geographical Society had bestowed on her its Founder's Medal, remarking particularly on her journey between Hureidha in the Wadi Hadhramaut to the sea. 'Her success', read the nomination, 'has been due to her courage, determination, and, above all, to her gift for making friends with all types and conditions of peoples.'

She was also living the kind of life she really liked best, surrounded by experts and soldiers and scholars, all driven by a common purpose. Freya always admired soldiers. She liked their 'impression of calmness and efficient leisure'. She paid attention to what they said, and made allowances for them that she would never have made for civilians. She looked for the soldier-scholar in them all. She saw it in Wavell and in General Wilson, whose eyes, she once said, were like those of an elephant, 'small, shrewd and wise'. She was, said her friends, very like a soldier herself, thinking tactical thoughts and strategies of Empire.

CHAPTER SIX

Persuasion, not Propaganda

Freya's talents were now widely recognized to lie in propaganda, or, as she preferred to call it, persuasion. Among the generals she had become a celebrity – General Smuts was said to know parts of her books by heart – and at the Ministry of Information she had acquired a reputation for being able to talk to ordinary people in such a way that they believed what she said. There was something in her manner, stern, uncompromising, full of charm, using words that rang out with conviction and unmistakable probity, that was very attractive. From Cairo, Wavell was on record as saying that the Brotherhood had played an essential part in internal security and done much to lessen sabotage against the Allies in Egypt. What was more, Freya now had a wider following. For some time she had been writing regularly from the Near East for *The Times* articles that upheld Britain and her role as moral guide in a confused world. The time had perhaps come to give her a new audience.

By 1943 there was a strong agreement in official circles in Britain that the Zionists in Palestine should be helped as far as possible, but only with the consent of the Arabs.

Finding this historical attachment to the Arab world so entrenched, the Zionists had been shifting their campaign to the United States. They were now fighting Malcolm Macdonald's White Paper of 1939, in which he had proposed limiting Jewish immigration into Palestine to 75,000 in the next five years, and after that only if the Arabs agreed. Freya, whose understanding of the Arab position was thought to be acute, was now asked to go to America to lecture on the Middle East – largely on the premise that Americans had very little idea of what it was really like – because the Zionists were currently making British policy in Palestine much harder to enforce. Freya herself, having watched American interest in the area grow with that in oil, thought the time right.

She was not, perhaps, the most obvious of choices for the task, for all her travels and understanding. Freya had never been to America and her one encounter with the new world in Canada had left her a little scathing of its culture. More important, she has never been admiring of the Jews. From Haifa, in the summer of 1931, she had written to her father: 'I don't think anyone but a Jew can really like the Jews: they so obviously have no use for anyone else. Their manners are horrid compared to the Arab; and I felt, by the end of a day among them, that it is far better to be a Jew among the Philistines than an unlucky Philistine among the Jews.'

The tour started with a by now customary set-back to her health. Far out to sea, crossing the Atlantic on a crammed troopship, the *Aquitania*, Freya developed appendicitis. By the time she was carried to shore by stretcher at Halifax, through heavy rain, with the troops lining the railings watching, the appendix was rupturing. She was immediately operated on in the Halifax infirmary and, surviving by her usual combination of robustness and tenacity, she was soon sitting up and writing letters, tended by nuns. Though she lamented that she had lost a month, by November she was in New York, building up to a schedule of tea parties, lectures and dinners that would have crushed many younger and healthier women. The city enchanted her: 'I can't get over the exciting beauty,' she wrote, 'the pencil buildings so high and far that the blueness of the sky floats about them; the feeling that one's taxis, and shoppings all go on in the deep canyon-beds of natural erosions rather than in the excrescences of human builders.' After four years of war, the hats and lingerie of New York were particularly dazzling.

Within days of arriving Freya began contacting anti-Zionist Jews, to whom she spoke out firmly on the second clause of the Balfour Declaration ('It being clearly understood that nothing shall be done which may prejudice the civil and religious rights of existing non-Jewish communities in Palestine.'). Her view, and the one that she intended to carry up and down the country, was that the proposals outlined in the White Paper were far too important to the Arabs and to the stability of the Middle East to be tinkered with, and that it was up to the moderate Jews, because they too were interested in fighting Zionism, to co-operate with the British. She soon wrote to Elizabeth Monroe, her senior at the Ministry of Information, about a dinner organized in her honour: 'The distressing thing is that I *like* the Jews I meet here and have to argue with, almost better than anyone else I see, and there was a most disarming mixture of sharpness, kindness and humour about the rabbi.'

Not everyone did so well with her as the rabbi had done. At a dinner in New York, Freya was introduced to Clare Luce. Within minutes they had fallen into a discussion about India. Clare Luce observed that the British were behaving badly by failing to give an undertaking on independence; Freya countered by suggesting that she might like to float a new slogan, 'Freedom for Fratricide'. The exchange grew chilly. 'Let there be massacres,' declared Clare Luce. 'Why should the white races have a monopoly of murder?' To her friends, afterwards, Freya had the last word. 'If she carries much weight now,' she wrote of Clare Luce, 'I don't think she will in a few years; she is too much tinkle . . . and she makes the mistake, eventually fatal to lovely women, of antagonizing all the women.'

From this moment on, in fact, Freya's tour was often prickly. In a letter to Cockerell she reported that her days were spent dealing with 'slanders, envy, detraction and all malignancy as well as mere ignorance'. As usual, she was caught by the spectacle and distressed by man's abuse of it. From Chicago, where she had witnessed a snowstorm, she wrote of the 'skyscrapers in the background and the lake with blocks of ice making a white horizon . . . and inside the hotel it is like the Balkans grown prosperous – square short females with furs and cordial voices telling everyone's business in the lounge. It is immense fun – only appalling to think that these are the people who are to have a hand in the delicate and subtle East. Anyway, I believe it is ridiculous to try and pour culture like chocolate over an ice *on top of a nation* . . .'

Catching 'The Chief', the famed steel-and-aluminium East-to-West-Coast train, Freya moved on late in January to California, where she stayed with Lucy Beach, daughter of the Sylvia Beach who had run a silk factory in Asolo in the early years of the century, before turning it over to Flora, and the family friend with whom Flora had spent her last months. By now she was deeply disenchanted with America. 'I feel', she wrote mournfully to Pamela Hore-Ruthven, 'their civilization not only alien but dead and also have a horrid fear of it, that we may be infected and let ourselves be carried down this way of mechanical annihilation.' To Wavell, she complained: 'This is a monstrous country . . . I feel rather like a slightly discouraged David travelling across this land with one Goliath after another to meet, and only a small packet of slingstones which the Mogul perpetually begs one not to use . . .'

However ill at ease and hostile she felt, Freya clearly disguised it, for she was not disliked by the Americans in return. On the contrary, her particular style, forceful and gracious, and her English air of cultured certainty, went down very well among the ladies and on the platforms, where she had become a fluent speaker. Writing of Freya's reception in California, Lucy Beach remarked to a friend in London: 'You know I've not seen Freya for six years, and I found that she has grown very much. She has great poise and authority. But she is the same dear person, quite unspoiled . . .'

The tour ended in Boston, at the end of April. Apart from a brief visit to Canada, to see the farm her father had left her, Freya had been to New York, Washington, Chicago, Los Angeles, San Francisco, Boston and Newport. It was not easy for anyone to assess quite what she had achieved, though her visit had not passed unnoticed or unreported and two rabbis and a member of Congress had requested her removal.

In the House of Commons, Brendan Bracken, Minister of Information, was questioned by a Liberal M P called Geoffrey Mander as to whether Freya had been sent to the United States to spread pro-Arab propaganda. Brendan Bracken replied that she had gone at the invitation of the Oriental Institute of Chicago and that he would certainly put on record 'that she has nothing to do with propaganda for Arabs or anyone else'.

Freya herself had reached the conclusion that in the States the British technique over Palestine should be that of a relay race, with one Arab expert taking over when the last became too visible in the Zionist spotlight. She now planned to retire to the Devonshire moors to write a short and popular book on the Arab question. Her last official function was to give a talk on Boston radio; after which, to her chagrin and confirming all she felt about America, the announcer thanked her and promised listeners a 'circus of performing animals' for the next day.

Freya was never absolutely clear about the purpose of her next wartime occupation, a visit to India. In the autumn of 1944, having spent the summer months in a hotel in

Chagford writing *East is West*, she received an invitation
from Lady Wavell, since 1943 Vicereine of India, to go out
to Delhi, where a committee of the Women's Voluntary
Services had been formed to try and think up ways of in-
volving Indian women in the war. It had, wrote Lady
Wavell, a programme 'beyond me and anyway I haven't the
time'. The Wavells and Freya were by now good friends,
with affectionate letters passing regularly between her and
the Viceroy, who filled his pages with verse and doggerel,
both charming and funny. Lady Wavell was not a letter
writer. Though never at her best with women, and increasingly impatient with administration, Freya agreed,
asking only that she be allowed to return to Europe once
Italy was liberated. Before leaving she wrote to a friend,
Austin Harrison, that she hoped the new job was not going
to consist of running the W V S as 'my one aim and function
in life is to de-organize the organized, especially women.
Organization is becoming a sort of nightmare.'

Early in February 1945, Freya left England by flying boat
in the company of three generals, the party having been
delayed for nearly a week in Poole harbour by ice. She
reached Delhi when the weather was at its best, hot days,
cold nights; the roses were out; the gardens of the Viceroy's
house had been opened to the public and were full of
'families, which makes them cheerful . . . astonishingly like
a Persian miniature, especially when the *chuprassis* with a
pointed cap sticking up from their turban and scarlet coats
come wandering by'. The Wavells were away, so Freya
joined the amateur artists and went painting with one of
the A D Cs, Billy Henderson. In the afternoons she made

excursions to photograph a palace or a temple, or visited the bazaar, to bargain for a piece of jewellery or early coin.

It was not, in fact, her first visit to India. In February 1943, wishing for a break from the Brothers and Sisters of Freedom, Freya had come to spend a few weeks with the Wavells; she had liked what she saw, approving of the 'solid Victorian feeling – everything *good*, nothing of careless rapture'. Something of a mystery surrounds the end of that visit. Freya had expressed a wish to drive from Delhi to Tehran and on Wavell's orders a car had been found for her. Whether she bought it, as she always claims, or was only lent it, as others maintain, when she reached Tehran she sold it, at an enormous profit, a transaction greatly frowned on by officials from one end of the Near East to the other – cars were in acutely short supply. (Another version had it that the car had belonged to the MoI, and that after being rebuked, Freya cabled London with the words from Rudyard Kipling's 'If': 'If you can make one heap of all your winnings and risk it on the turn of pitch and toss . . .') The affair had been put down to Freya's unique mixture of mild unscrupulousness and disregard for officialdom; in Delhi it was the subject of many affectionate jokes.

When the Wavells returned to Viceroy House immense formality came with them. Though Wavell was a very different figure from his predecessor, Lord Linlithgow, and as easygoing as the former Viceroy had been orderly, as representative of the King there could be no relaxation from the most rigid attention to etiquette. Matters of rank, title and precedence were presided over by four ADCs, two of whom were always on duty; curtseying and bowing were compulsory and at the end of State dinners the ladies left the dining room in pairs, pausing at the far end of the hall to form up and curtsey. Freya remarked that curtseying had a 'devastating effect on conversation' and that splendour cast a blight, 'a loveless thing that the human soul has difficulty in digging its roots into'.

Her words were somewhat disingenuous. Freya liked pageantry and grandeur; this was her sort of place. For all the complaints that she found it hard to discuss *Hamlet* among a lot of silent ADCs, ceremonial was always something she much enjoyed. Lutyens' Viceroy House, last of the great palaces of its kind, was not exactly beautiful, with its sandwich-like layers of cream and reddish stone; nor was it precisely comfortable, with marble corridors the length of railway stations, so poorly lit there had to be artificial light all day, while the trees in the garden were expressly pruned low, on Lutyens' orders, so that guests had to carry their chairs round with them from one patch of shade to another. But life within had all that Freya desired. There were 300 servants. She had a pleasant set of rooms and ate whenever at home with the Wavells, whether informally in the small dining room, occasions on which she excelled, for Wavell had no small talk, and wished only really to discuss poetry, military history and golf, the first two of which were ideal for her; or on State occasions, when a turbanned servant stood behind every chair. It was at one of these banquets that she found herself seated next to Mountbatten. She considered him very good-looking, but was distressed when she realized that he was totally uninterested in her, coming to life only when two pet cranes were brought in to be fed.

'True British trait,' she remarked a little sourly, 'to prefer animals to conversation.'

Increasingly, however, Freya was invited out. Wartime Delhi, like Cairo and Baghdad, was very gay. Once again, Freya was a particular success among the young soldiers on leave in the several camps around the city. At one dance, Lady Wavell went to some length to gather a decent number of attractive young girls. The soldiers clustered around Freya, who, having hurt her knee scrambling over a temple, lay reclining like Madame Récamier on a sofa. Billy Henderson was sent over to disperse the crowd. Ten minutes later they were back at Freya's feet.

Those who knew Freya in Delhi all speak of her clothes. Billy Henderson recalls with particular clarity a lemon-coloured raw-silk suit, with a coat worn rather long over the skirt; on her head, Freya had placed a pheasant, a bird made into a hat. Peter Coats, controller before him, wrote in his autobiography *Of Generals and Gardens*, that her 'poke bonnets, aprons and a hat with a clock-face on the crown were second only to Gandhi's fast as a topic of conversation'. Certainly she made their lives more fun. She enticed them out to take her for drives or to visit buildings they had never even heard of. And her obvious delight in picnics – especially in Simla, staying in Viceroy Lodge, when large parties, waited on by footmen, would gather among the rhododendrons in the hills – infected all around her.

Freya was in Simla for the June conference with Gandhi and Nehru, having driven up overnight with Billy Henderson in his open Austin Seven, stopping at dawn for breakfast in a maharajah's garden in the foothills. Though

she had, of course, no official role, her charm and forth-
comingness pleased the Indians, who had already been
much disconcerted by Wavell's lack of conversation, and,
wrote Coats, 'her tact and quick wit . . . glossed over some
awkward moments. Her clothes, dirndls, sun bonnets,
Tibetan aprons and Jaipur jewellery . . . a constant joy.'
Though even Freya could do little on one occasion when
Lady Wavell, emerging from a day-dream, announced to
Nehru over tea that she hated circuses because of the captive
animals. 'Captive?' said Nehru, who had come to the conference straight from a British gaol. 'Yes,' said Lady Wavell,
vaguely, unaware of everyone's frantic but wholly unsuccessful efforts to start up another topic. 'Behind bars,
you know.' 'Yes,' said Nehru.

As for the work, it remained very hard to describe precisely what Freya did. She did travel down to the south, on
a regal outing of her own, staying in residencies, meeting
rajahs and British ladies, tasting the last of the great Victorian Anglo-Indian splendours. And evidently her talks
were admired, for Wavell wrote to her: 'You don't know
what a success you have been with the people you have met
since you arrived in India. On all hands I have been congratulated on getting you to help.' By mid-April, however,
she was complaining that she had been thrown 'as it were
into the arms of philanthropy, for which I have a natural
repugnance unless its stern features relax into some human
face'. She now concluded that what was needed was a group
of four salaried women and a clerk, with a voluntary
committee in Delhi to act on their recommendations, while
the women 'goodwill messengers', as she named them,

93

travelled, making contact with women working all over the country. What, precisely, these women were meant to be working at was never explained. Of her own role, Freya was later to say only that it had been a 'happy unproductive half year'. By July she was off, having watched the progress of liberation across Europe and into Northern Italy. 'Freya left,' wrote Billy Henderson in his diary. 'Alas. Alas.'

Freya had entered the war a traveller and a writer. She emerged from it a public figure, widely regarded throughout the Arab world, a friend to Cabinet Ministers and generals. Those who had not seen her for six years found her greatly changed. 'I look at her in astonishment,' wrote Mrs Granville to Lady Lawrence, two family friends, 'for she has so improved with years. She is *much* better looking. She is a little stouter and somehow it suits her, but she has such an air of assurance, a woman of the world accustomed to being made much of, *and* she looks so much happier . . . There is not a line on her face . . . She does look very foreign, but of course she is . . . the last garment I asked about was made in Delhi when she was staying with the Wavells. Her jewels, lots of them – were very foreign and her coat was a goatskin from Cyprus.'

Some of this, of course, was the confidence that came from being consulted and listened to and from work which had been visibly successful: in Cairo, especially, the Brothers of Freedom had become a well-established movement (and was to remain so, until disbanded with the abrogation of the Anglo-Egyptian Treaty, when fighting broke out in the Canal Zone in 1952). Freya was now fifty-two. Six years of attention and command had strengthened her. Her style, in speech as in writing, had become more definite, her views more pronounced. She could now, complained a friend, be haughty.

More importantly perhaps, six years of war had made her an extraordinary number of friends, not only among great men, but with a younger generation of Middle East experts, who were to become constant companions and guests. Whether in Baghdad or Tehran, Cairo or Delhi, she had been fêted and admired in the very world she liked best, that of soldiers and statesmen. Many of her friends regard those years as the best of her life. The attention would have pleased anyone; for Freya, after such solitary struggle, it was comforting to be so prized. Not surprisingly, perhaps, her spirits now dropped a little. 'What', she wrote apprehensively to Cockerell, 'shall I do with myself after the war?'

CHAPTER SEVEN

Marriage

Freya returned to Asolo to find herself regarded, not altogether admiringly, as a spy. What else, the villagers seemed to imply, could she possibly have been doing as a woman during five years of war in the Near East? Her reception was friendly, but a little wary. Caroly Piaser, who had met Freya briefly before the war, and who had run Flora's silk factory in her absence, turning it over to more practical wartime work, could remember only that before leaving for London in 1939, Freya had said to her: 'We'll meet again in 1945. We'll stay poor; but we won't lose the war.'

The Asolani were indeed poor. Everywhere there was hunger, intense dreariness; the valleys were full of burnt-out houses and people felt extremely bitter about forty-eight local young men, hanged on the trees of nearby Bassano as the SS pulled out. To make things worse, in the middle of August, a hailstorm, accompanied by a sudden tornado, destroyed all crops, including the tomatoes and fruit. There was very little to eat.

Early on in the war Casa Freia had been taken over by six

fascist generals, who cut down the laurels by the front door to make a field of fire against the partisans advancing up the road. But in comparison with neighbours' houses, which had been ransacked of all their furniture, the place had been barely touched. Freya arrived home in time for the peace celebrations of 25 August. She borrowed a very faded Union Jack to hang alongside the Italian flags in the street, and joined a group of young British theologians, studying to become priests while they waited for demobilization, for 'Te Deum' in the church. Objecting that the civilian food ration was not sufficient to keep a mouse alive, she started a successful system of barter with local peasants; a farmer promised honey, a herdsman a little butter. Corn was obtained by ferrying black-market sacks across the Po at night. For the moment, Freya had much to occupy her, and, as she wrote to Wavell's daughter Felicity: 'I am having a reaction against Work which makes it impossible almost to do anything at all except potter around the garden, deciding where to plant stocks and delphiniums.'

In any case, her war was not quite over. In October the Ministry of Information offered her a car, a driver and £100 a month to travel around the towns of northern Italy and set up reading centres, with English magazines and books, to restore a spirit of warmth to Anglo-Italian relations. Her boss was Michael Stewart, Political Attaché in Rome; he gave her 'the pride of the fleet', a car captured from the Germans. (It was later stolen from her by two GIs.)

Complaining a bit that she had been 'badgered' into it, Freya was none the less pleased to be on the move, not least, perhaps, because she hoped to do better for the British in Italy than they had done for themselves in the Middle East. There, she reflected dispiritedly, they had failed because of their want of conviction in what they were saying, and their 'neglect of disinterested service'.

Early in December she set out for Bolzano, Merano, Bressanone and Trento; two weeks later it was Cremona, Milan and Turin. Wherever she stopped, she gave little speeches, and talked to local priests and school teachers about the need to build up Culture and not ignore the Left. The weather was dismal, with thick fog; the roads were sometimes impassable, pitted beyond use by armoured vehicles. But the trips were not without fun. Freya had developed a taste for Marmora powdered marble, and asked a new friend, Osbert Lancaster, to come with her to study the baroque churches in order to design marble baroque bathrooms for Casa Freia. Lulie Abul Huda, a visitor at the same time, went with them. In each new town, Osbert Lancaster would set off with one Baedeker towards a baroque building, Lulie Abul Huda with another in search of renaissance churches, while Freya, laden with pamphlets, went off to teach the Italians about democracy. Her mission of persuasion accomplished, she would join them in the café, saying what a good meeting it had been, and off they would go to a delicious lunch of rich northern black-market food, all the sweeter for the austerity of Asolo.

The job lasted six months. Freya celebrated the true end to war with a walk in the Dolomites, her first climb for over twelve years. Her legs ached, but she was relieved to find that she could still do it.

Both *East is West* and her mother's *An Italian Diary* were out and selling. Freya now needed a new book. Pausing in Paris for a first post-war Schiaparelli dress, explaining that 'I am sure the way to enjoy life is to live in obscurity with frequent escapades,' she reached London in October to talk to Jock Murray. What she had in mind was a collection of essays, her 'own Everywoman philosophy', to be called *Perseus in the Wind*, on themes 'beyond our grasp, yet visible to all, dear to our hearts and far from our understanding as the constellations, a comfort for the frail light they shed'. 'You must first have something you wish to say and then you must say it,' she had told a gathering in Baghdad some years before. 'But it must be what *you* want to say. Courage is the first virtue of style; the courage of one's own belief.' There was much Freya now wished to say; and she had never lacked courage.

First, though, she had finance to arrange. Six years of war had freed her from continual anxiety about money. Back in Europe, with a longing to decorate her house and buy herself new clothes from the Paris collections, she needed to find a new way to bring in an income. What she wanted first, however, was a fur coat.

To Jock Murray, she now put what appeared to her an extremely sensible proposal: £4,000 immediately for a mink coat, in return for the copyright to all her books when she died. Already somewhat in disgrace for being less than totally enthusiastic about *Perseus*, he now fell further by appearing dubious, protesting that it would surely be unsafe to own such a coat. The board at Murray's were altogether more sceptical. They vetoed the mink and offered £1,500. Freya crossly turned it down, saying she felt like Julius

Caesar when the pirates asked too little ransom. 'I have decided,' she wrote to a Baghdad friend, Gerald de Gaury, 'never to save anything *ever*, and to collect things that are beautiful and precious whenever I can as a protest against this dreary evenness.'

In September, Stewart Perowne sent Freya a telegram asking her to marry him. She replied accepting. Stewart was being sent by the Foreign Office to Antigua and the plan was that as soon as her marble bathrooms in Asolo were in place she would go out to join him. On the 14th, she wrote to Nigel Clive, her p.g. in Baghdad. 'Such a peculiar thing has happened: I have promised to marry Stewart. I have not written to anyone to tell them yet; but I must say so at once to you, for you are very dear to me, nor do I feel that this or anything else will affect it . . . It is one of the happy things that Stewart likes the people I like. We have a common world to set out in.'

Not all Freya's friends were surprised. For all her brave words to Venetia Buddicom in the early thirties – 'Life is easier for married people: but I think it ought if anything to be richer for us, so long as we take it with full hands and not with the inferiority sense which has often ruined the lives of spinsters' – Freya had always wanted to marry. Fretted over by her mother, obsessed often by feelings of being plain and unattractive, she had returned again and again in letters to the theme of being alone. True, Freya was now fifty-four, Stewart forty-six. But he was charming, witty, a good Arabist, and could expect, if not an embassy, at least some fairly prestigious Foreign Office posting. What was more, as she pointed out, they shared a common world.

The marriage took place in London, in October, and a crowded reception was held at John Murray's at 50 Albemarle Street, in the room in which Byron's letters had been burned. Jock Murray gave her away. Freya, deep at work on *Perseus*, had just finished a chapter on love. The couple returned to Asolo, to a house filled with tube roses. By the 25th Stewart was off to Barbados and Freya began arranging her life so that she could join him. To Cockerell, she expressed some alarm at what she had done: had it been possible, she wrote, 'I would have done like an unwilling horse at a jump and taken the nearest gap in the nearest hedge.'

To anyone she was fond of, Freya had always written letters. Stewart now became her daily confidant. Evidently he was a poor correspondent, for soon she was complaining that she had no news of him. Uncertain about what to wear in post-war colonial gatherings, she announced that she had packed five big straw hats, four parasols, two fans and some mittens. When a letter came, it expressed concern about money. Freya replied sternly: 'I *never will* devote to Ordinary Life' the extra income from a book. 'It is the stuff one's dreams are made of and, however poor I have been, I have always devoted it to dreams.'

By early February 1948, Freya had reached Bridgetown, pleased to be able to report that the half white coral, half dark lava island was pretty and sweet smelling. But Barbados was not Freya's sort of place, nor was her role, that of wife to a middle-ranking member of the colonial office, likely to satisfy her. After nearly a decade of public admiration and attention, polite conversation with diplomatic wives who had never heard of her was not enjoyable. By the end of the month, she was writing sadly to Jock Murray of a 'sort of caged feeling'. Stewart, she said, had been turned into the perfect civil servant. 'I do think there is an element of *darkness* in the Government Service; it makes people think themselves important, a *frightful* thing to do.'

Freya did not enjoy Barbados, nor was she happy with Stewart. In April, she decided to go home, hoping to patch things up with Stewart later. Her letters to him from Asolo were subdued; as the months went by they became warmer, less accusatory, as if, separated from him physically, she could again believe in the romance of their late marriage. 'Do you know,' she wrote to him in July, 'that all my life I have lived in a sort of Eden, with no sense of personal insecurity (moral I mean) or danger? Now since marrying you I have suddenly become aware of how precious it all is.'

Perseus in the Wind, twenty essays on such themes as beauty, death, and sorrow, not unlike her earlier essays from Baghdad, but more literary and more assertive in tone, was now out, to a very mixed reception. Wavell wrote to say that it was 'like a casket not of jewellery ... but of pieces of jewellery with jewels in beautiful or quaint or cunning settings and often so pleasantly unexpected'. Others were less admiring: 'May we not feel,' asked one reviewer, 'that if we are going to have almost unadulterated Great Thoughts for 169 pages they ought to be very great indeed?'

Freya had now started work on her autobiography, sorting and bringing together the immensely long personal letters she had written to Cockerell from Cyprus in 1942

when she referred to all she had forgotten as 'strips of black
unfathomable water between ships'. Cockerell, who greatly
enjoyed managing people, spurred her on. On her wedding
anniversary, 7 October, Freya sent Stewart a telegram: 'Love
to you darling and many thoughts, particularly today.'

In Asolo, Freya settled to a way of life that suited her
perfectly. She had friends to stay, people she had not seen
since before the war, and her newer Middle Eastern col-
leagues, coming to Asolo for the first time. There were expeditions to show them the Palladian villas along the Po,
evenings at the Fenice in Venice, picnics in the Dolomites.
In the evenings, guests played Scrabble, over camomile tea,
or grappa, the fiery spirit of Northern Italy, which Freya, no
drinker herself, considered as settling as a tisane. Increasingly, she blamed Barbados for the difficulties of their marriage; what she and Stewart needed, she told friends, was a
posting to the East 'big enough for one to keep one's own
scale of values'.

On good terms again, Freya was writing to him almost
daily. In October she outlined her perfect day: 'a fine
morning, all alone, walk with Checchi round the garden,
post arrives and then three hours spent over the writing of
English (the article is done and goes by surface). A little
meditation after lunch under the wistaria, looking at the
Japanese anemones now like a white and pink halo round
the pool, and then a heavenly walk all by myself for one and
a half hours in and out of the slopes of the Rocca . . . It was
a day sweet and heavy like honey, a white sky, and all the
country sounds, voices and laughter, animals, the crackling
noise of carts in the plain below . . . Rory Cameron came

over to find refuge from what he calls "the hard glitter of Italian hospitality" and sat for one and a half hours talking about India and Moguls and Hickey, very agreeably. And then a bath and a little chat to you, and soon dinner.' There was Caroly Piaser next door in the silk factory, to talk desultory business with; in the house itself Emma, the cook, who had come to Freya as a young maid just before the war, and her husband Checchi, the gardener. It was a pleasing and solid routine, and if Freya was at the same time worrying at doubts it was in her disciplined nature to keep them firmly suppressed. Most revealing, perhaps, are the passages for *Traveller's Prelude* that she was writing at about this time concerning her mother, when she came to marry her father in remote Dartmoor in 1880: 'It is far better to know the limits of one's resistance at once and put up as it were a little friendly fence around the private ground.'

One day, she carried the first three chapters of her book over to Bernard Berenson at I Tatti in Fiesole and read them aloud to him after dinner by the fire. Berenson fell deeply asleep. Freya was both cross and amused. He 'bore this sad lugubrious symptom out by saying that he thinks this sort of book (plain chronological) not very exciting', she reported despondently to Jock Murray. 'I have an awful *feel* he may be right.'

Stewart appeared in Asolo for Christmas. The roses and jasmine were out and the weather blue and crisp. There were charades and parties in the local villas, occasions on which Stewart, funny, erudite, speaking several languages, shone. Marina Volpi, the friend who had got Flora out of prison in 1942 and whom Freya had once approvingly described as a 'fascinating neighbour with dark purple fingernails and tiny Russian boots and high heels', gave her customary sumptuous Christmas dinner under the Veronese frescoes of Maser, preceded by Mass in the little chapel at the bottom of the drive. Dinner ended at three. Freya had bought a Vespa, to the concern of the Asolani, for she had no notion of how to stop, and went off to dinner parties, in long Arab dress, covered in jewels, confident that a manservant would be at the door to catch the machine and control it before she tumbled off. Freya was outraged when Marina Volpi, as outspoken as Freya with her friends, declared before a large gathering: 'You are a marvellous writer, but you drive like a dog.'

In the New Year, Freya and Stewart, who shared a sense of adventure as well as many friends, set off for a tour of Tuscany by Vespa, despite heavy snow. Freya regarded it as an excellent substitute for a horse, able to tackle much the same sort of country, and was furious when ice forced them to take to the trains.

Both Stewart and Freya had close and concerned friends in official circles. Efforts to find him another post, better suited to both their lives, had evidently been made, for when they reached Rome there was a telegram informing him that he was to be sent to Benghazi in Cyrenaica, under British rule since the end of the war. It was Arab-speaking, little visited and covered in Roman and Greek remains. Freya went with him, taking furniture and books. The Vespa was to travel out behind.

In 1950, what is now Libya was split into two,

Tripolitania, prosperous and lively, and Cyrenaica, a long strip of rather barren coastline. In each was a British resident, and a number of British advisers. Cyrenaica, however, also had Emir Idris, who was to be King of Libya once the two areas were merged and given a constitution; a fragile man in his late fifties with a drooping white moustache and laceless tennis shoes.

Benghazi, on the sea, was a town of little distinction apart from a few streets of Italian colonial architecture. It had taken two years to clear the rubble of the war and many of the houses were still in ruins. Nevertheless, Freya was delighted: 'all the cheerful squalor, the gay dishevelled dirt and beauty mixed of the East, the dazzle of the sea so much more brilliant than any other'. The Perownes had been allocated one of a row of semi-detached houses, near to the head of Chancery. Freya took one look and refused it. Catching sight, across the harbour, of a collection of more isolated houses, she found one to be vacant. It had a garden, and a well, but no staircase, so the interior was gutted to fit one in. Here, late in April, on what had been a hideous fascist sideboard, relic of an Italian predecessor, she started work on the second volume of her autobiography, *Beyond Euphrates*, stopping occasionally to take the Vespa for a spin into Benghazi. The measured, reflective tone shows how far she was now able to distance life from the discipline of work, though even in the most considered of philosophical statements something of her new anxieties was apparent. 'It is wise', she was writing, 'to discover what our happiness is made of. Of the ingredients of which mine is made I think the presence of goodness comes first, and the affection of a few people I can understand and care about is second. The third is sunshine. After these and close upon them, comes some sort of daily beauty, preferably a spacious view; and after that and side by side – expressions perhaps of the same desire – domestic servants of an old-fashioned friendly sort, and an atmosphere of sequence in time, a regular procession and not a disorderly scramble towards eternity. I like to have as much as possible of the background of this procession in sight, and could never live happily for long in a country where no winding footpaths have been made by the steps of my predecessors . . . I think that these pleasures – all receptive – are more essential to me than my own work. They mean more than any applause or esteem, for the voice of other people only touches if it carries affection; and I can imagine nothing more barren than to be admired and not loved.'

Cyrenaica was not easy for Stewart. A backwater in career terms, and regarded in the Foreign Office as an agreeable and not over-strenuous post, it had been efficiently administered for some years by a group of advisers all of whom had carefully mapped out their patches and made their contacts. Stewart, as chief adviser to the Minister of the Interior, was, remembers a colleague, 'a bit of a fifth wheel on a coach'. Soon he was pining nostalgically for Baghdad, where his epigrams were admired and his laughing easy manner had made him many friends. But in more ways it was harder for Freya. She was in her late fifties; her style, her tastes, her interests were all fixed: she enjoyed travel in rough places, and the remote desert and mountain people, and she valued the company of those like herself, travellers, scholars,

writers. Benghazi was not a fashionable place. The civil
servants posted there were often very nice, but they were
rarely very amusing. A strong air of cosy respectability hung
over the town. Freya was never good in suburbia. 'The only
way to survive was to muck in,' says Lavender Goddard-
Wilson, who became a friend. Freya did not muck in. It was
not exactly that she felt superior; she simply had no talent
for it. Sitting near her at gatherings, Lavender Goddard-
Wilson would watch her eyes, missing nothing, what Peter
Coats in India had called her ability to play 'oculist to a
hawk'.

For their part, the foreign community were somewhat
baffled by Freya; most had never heard of her and knew
little about the Middle East, having come to Cyrenaica from
the Sudan. They looked on her, kindly but with no admiration, as a little odd in shape and appearance.

Whenever they could, the Perownes got away. In under
an hour's drive they could be in marvellous country, on
sites described by Herodotus. At weekends they went to
Cyrene, 1,000 feet above the plain, the great city where
baths, temples and a theatre had been dug by Italians. One
day, Freya went fox-hunting on the Barce plain with the
16th Lancers. To friends who had lost husbands or sons in
the desert war, she wrote describing the battlefields, the
derelict tanks and armoured cars still littering the sand. In
May, Wavell died. 'It leaves a great hole in life,' she wrote to
Cockerell, 'one of the great men gone and there are not so
many.'

It was obvious now that the marriage was not going
well. When out on picnics, or dining with friends, it was

Stewart who held forth on the antiquities; Freya, uncharacteristically, seemed increasingly withdrawn. Away from him, her letters were reproachful: 'Hope you are happier on your own! I felt I was just in the way.' And, on another occasion, 'I came away sadly yesterday – sad, sad reasons. It is towards the end of life, so perhaps it doesn't matter.' Apart for a while, Freya's letters would grow fond again.

In the summer of 1951 the post of British adviser to the Ministry of the Interior in Benghazi was suddenly eliminated. Stewart was temporarily without a job. Then a short position, advising the British delegates to the United Nations on Arab affairs, came up. With some misgivings, Freya accompanied him to Paris. While Stewart was at the Palais de Chaillot, Freya went to drawing classes, and yearned after a Dessé grey evening 'gown scarfed with black chiffon and held in a sort of milky way of diamond stars'. She had not lost her sharpness. Deeply scathing of the United Nations, she remarked to Nigel Clive: 'I don't want ever any more to do Public Things. I want to make a good end.'

By that summer the marriage was over. It was a bitter time for Freya. She had hoped, perhaps even convinced herself, that she would be able to mould a satisfactory marriage out of what had certainly been a good friendship with Stewart and that at last she would have one person in the world who would belong to her. But Stewart was not mouldable, nor was he, as he himself remarked, Prince Albert. She felt it most strongly because she saw it as a profound failure, of a kind she could not quite understand or accept; so long a practitioner of will, she was not used to failure. Once more, as after her mother had died, she now felt in a 'room far too big for one'.

'He doesn't want *me*, he wants a home and a lot of odds and ends,' she wrote to Nancy Astor. 'But marriage is more than that . . . Friendship is as far as the thermometer will rise, and there it must rest for the present.' She stated that she would give up the name Perowne; it would be Stark again, Mrs Stark this time.

CHAPTER EIGHT

In Search of Alexander

Freya was not given to self-recrimination, nor did she ever permit herself the luxury of prolonged despondency. Travel had always worked well for her; it would work well again, and this time it would be in a new part of the world. The Arab East now receded, and she was rarely to go back there again, except on visits to friends; Asia Minor was about to take over. To the new continent she brought all the enthusiasm and sense of adventure that had filled her as she set sail from Venice, bound for Brummana, almost thirty years earlier.

Before setting off, before even mapping out the routes and goals that characterized every journey, Freya arrived in London for a grand tour. It was to be exhausting, meeting friends and acquaintances without break, but it was possibly the best of all the London seasons, and it set a style and a pattern for the yearly visits to follow.

It began with receiving an honorary doctorate from Glasgow University. Academic receptions, full of cultured and leisurely good conversation, robed ceremonial, the sense of timeless ritual, all this was what Freya liked best in British

life, and she paused in Paris on the way for a number of
suitable outfits. The three days of festivities over, she looked
in on the Scottish islands, then set off south for a round of
friends. There was Sissinghurst, where she found Vita
Nicolson wandering around in orange trousers, with a
wolfhound at her heels; Hatfield House, where she compared
breakfast conversation with Lord Salisbury to a 'thor-
oughbred horse, always pushing on anxious to find where
you want to go and to go there'; to Cliveden, where an
unhappy Nancy Astor told her she wanted to become a
saint, so that everyone might feel her influence when she
came into a room; and then to Windsor, to the Gowries,
Pamela Hore-Ruthven's father-in-law, Lieutenant-Governor
and Deputy Constable of Windsor Castle. In between came a
lunch in Henley, with Peter and Celia Fleming. 'One's friends
are wonderfully good,' Freya noted.

Then, at the beginning of a wet August week, came a
final visit to Houghton Hall in Norfolk, to stay with the
Marchioness of Cholmondeley, a close friend of Cockerell's
whom she had recently met with Duff and Diana Cooper at
the British Embassy in Paris. At Houghton, Freya commented, 'there is not the tremendous sense of history of
Hatfield, but a pleasant liveableness of civilization'. (It was
Lady Cholmondeley who suggested to her that she should
wear a lace cap, as in the eighteenth century, and she wore
one ever after.)

On her second day, Queen Mary came to tea. Freya was
always a keen student of clothes and grandeur; her regard
for royalty was like that for Empire, somewhat unquestioning. In a letter to Stewart she described the scene; if a

little much, a bit too admiring, it has none the less the same precision, the same sure eye, that she had brought to her tales of harem life in Baghdad. 'Queen Mary came at 4.20 and left at 7.15. She was very erect in grey glacé kid shoes, the kind of 1910 with little waisted heels; and a Liberty silk of pink flowers on pale blue under a pale blue coat with little cape, and pale blue marabou; a high tulle collar of the sort held up with whalebone; a pearl necklace, diamond brooch and earrings of a little diamond and huge pearls; a very pink make-up, and blonde-grey hair nicely waved; and a pale blue toque with a bunch of pink and yellow primulas and a white narcissus among them; and a grey silk parasol with a Fabergé handle of crystal and diamonds. She came along very anxious not to get her feet wet, with Lady Wyndham (whom I had met years ago at Petworth) very dowdy behind her with untidy hair. Perhaps a Lady-in-Waiting ought to be a little dowdy?' (In Freya's eyes there was never much charity towards a royal servant.)

More, certainly, than the pleasure in grandeur of this English tour, was the reaffirmation of friendships. Marriage had been a failure; friends were not. Freya, more keenly than anyone, understood about friends; she knew how well they had to be looked after, how constantly tended. Lord David Cecil, who had met her regularly since their encounter at Petworth in the thirties and had greatly come to value the way her 'sharp, observant mind tethered romanticism to reality', now counted her among the dozen or so people who had made the most impression on him. Some of this came from her attention to friendship. 'Like us,' he says, 'she always rated it very high. I don't know many people to

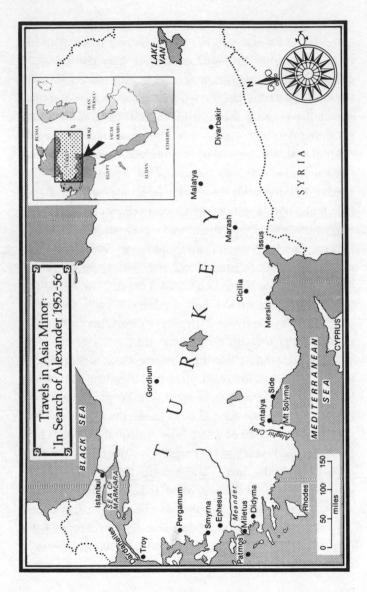

Travels in Asia Minor:
'In Search of Alexander' 1952-56

whom it meant as much as to her and to us. We had made friends because she was fascinating and unusual and because she wanted to. That's an essential condition.' Many others agree. Friendship with Freya could be demanding; she could be unprincipled, even merciless; but she was possessed of some rare quality that made people seek her out, and, once taken as a friend, many were willing to become devoted slaves. In return she made their lives seem somehow better. There was something about her unquestioning assumption that to be worthwhile people must be in control, and not ruled by circumstance, that made her approval very important.

On 4 September 1952 Freya boarded SS *Iskenderun* in Piraeus, heading for Smyrna on the west coast of Turkey, where she had a friend in David Balfour, the Consul-General, a former Greek Orthodox priest who took to diplomacy after concluding that 'man is just one of God's mistakes', and Seton Lloyd, who had been Director of the British Institute of Archaeology in Ankara since 1949. She had formed an idea that she would take Herodotus as her guide and visit the places he wrote about, to have a 'thread to run one's exploring on'. After a few days of wandering around sites she wrote tentatively to Jock Murray that it might even make a short book, *Talking with Herodotus*. 'Curiosity led me,' she was to explain, 'pure, disinterested curiosity, the human thrust in time.'

Freya was forming a pattern for her travels. Reading played a fundamental part, and before she had been in Turkey a fortnight she set off for Ankara, to spend some days with Seton and Ulrica Lloyd, reading in the Institute library. They remember her visit well. She was expected to arrive for lunch. One o'clock passed, with no sign of a taxi. The afternoon wore on. Then a message came to say that she was on her way. At nine, they sat down to dinner. At 9.30 a jeep stopped at the door. White with dust, stiff and bruised after fourteen hours of appalling roads, breakdowns, near crashes and unexplained delays, Freya stumbled up the stairs. The Lloyds made to usher her straight to a bath and bed, preparing themselves for a recital of travel disasters. Freya brushed them aside; finding the food still laid, she settled briskly in her place, put her elbows on the table, and began to talk of Alexander. She had come to Ankara to discuss history, and discuss it she would.

It was a good time to be in Turkey. The weather was excellent, travel was cheap and Turkish teachers easy to find. (On her own, Freya practised Turkish using translations of the Bible and Eric Ambler.) In October, David Balfour asked her to go with him to Patmos and Rhodes on his five-ton motor ketch *Elphin* and Freya set off gladly, with all the delight of a fresh departure. For a month they toured the islands, swimming by day, talking history at night. She left the *Elphin* to wander in the lower Meander Valley, then travelled on to Ephesus, Didyma and Miletus. She was planning a third book of essays, based on landscapes and ruins. On 11 November she wrote to Jock Murray: 'I begin to feel it is absolutely necessary to travel to Asia Minor. Rome and even Athens are stops on the way, but here is the source of all that has made us, all the ideas, all the patterns. And these Ionians seem to have been unaware that other human beings might want their world ... I do like barbarians on the whole.'

Freya again was on her own, walking, hiring jeeps or taxis, and even occasionally a pony. The weather turned very cold; the Meander flooded. Undeterred, she kept going; she regretted only, she told friends, the absence of a little danger, such a stimulating ingredient in Arab travel and sadly lacking in Turkey. The Lloyds, observing her progress, were overwhelmed by her doggedness, her absolute refusal to give in or complain, though frequently uncomfortable, unable to make herself understood and totally alone. A friend who joined up with her briefly during one of the stages in her route remembers her 'long baggy pants, a long Russian coat tied up with a golden cord and a pink umbrella, trotting through the rain, indestructibly brave'.

At the beginning of December she moved on to Cyprus, to stay with her architect friend Austen Harrison, from where she wrote to tell Lady Cholmondeley that she had visited fifty-five ancient Greek sites and cities in less than three months and encountered only one other fellow tourist, at Pergamum. To Jock Murray, she reported, 'Really this autumn has been very happy, spent with men (which I like) in real friendliness and nothing further. How restful and agreeable, and one of the pleasures of age to enjoy friendship undisturbed by oneself or others. One doesn't need anything very passionate, but just the gentleness of life, the eye that looks pleased when you enter, the feeling that there is no barrier.'

The serenity was real, but she could not always keep it up. Asolo, on her own, she found particularly hard. She was

there, alone, on her sixtieth birthday and though at work,
in an intensely self-disciplined way, on *Ionia: a Quest*, an
account of her autumn travels with Herodotus, she was
again worrying about money. As usual, Jock Murray, the
most devoted and constant of friends was the recipient of
her reproaches about the inconstancy of people, just as he
was, in letters to others, made the villain when she felt in
need of consolation. 'Jock', she wrote, after one of his visits,
to Pamela Hore-Ruthven (now Cooper, having just re-
married), 'was so overworked and strained . . . a state when
all intimacy goes, because one is always being warned off
the things that come naturally. How few people seem to
realize that friendship really does mean talking about the
things that one is *feeling* and with no guard, so that one can
for that little interval banish fear from one's daily life.' As a
friend, Freya could be exorbitant in her demands; those who
knew her well now sensed her acute loneliness in a new
and sometimes fretful tone. Postponed visits, letters not
answered quickly enough provoked stern rebukes.

There were few periods of unhappiness in her life out of
which Freya was not able to travel, and write, her way.
Ionia: a Quest was completed at great speed and, deeply
relieved, saying that she felt like a Victorian mother marrying off a daughter, she sent off the manuscript to Jock
Murray, and set her mind resolutely on an eight-month
absence in Asia Minor. Alexander, mentioned over the table
in Ankara to Seton Lloyd, had taken hold of her. 'I
wanted', she said later, 'to discover what Alexander found
in men's minds when he marched down from the Granicus
in 334 BC.'

But first she felt she had to learn good Turkish. By February 1954 she was back in Crete, studying several hours each day. Soon after, she reached the Turkish coast, at Issus, imagining the battle as it unfolded, the troops, the cavalry, the 'wide grey bed where Alexander and his white-plumed helmet pushed in with his guard about him ...' These were soldiers as she admired them most, who 'thought fighting natural and liked it'. What she was enjoying doing was conjuring up history in its rightful settings, relating what she read to what she saw, in bold sweeps that took in men, their characters and their campaigns. It was something new for her, and as it made its way into her writing, it rapidly found admirers.

In June came one of her more unsuccessful journeys. Misfortune took, as it often did with Freya, the shape not of the landscape, which rarely failed her, but that of a fellow traveller, whose ways she found uncongenial. The feeling was mutual.

Not long after the war had ended, Bernard Berenson had introduced Freya to a young painter called Derek Hill. He was fascinated by her and found her very charming. They talked about architecture and history. When, some four years later, she was planning her long tour of Turkey, she met him again at I Tatti and they agreed to make part of the journey together, to Marash and Malatya, so that Derek Hill could look at Armenian churches and Freya pursue Alexander. Berenson was sceptical. In the hall of I Tatti, they laid out the divided tent that they intended to share, with much laughter.

Early in June they met in Mersin. Even the start was

inauspicious. Derek Hill was late, having had his passport
stolen – a piece of inefficiency Freya always found hard to
excuse. Over dinner the first night, Derek Hill told her he
thought he would keep a diary, perhaps write something
about the journey. 'A glacial expression descended over her
face,' he remembers. 'No, Derek,' she said. 'I think that
would be very rude to me. I am the writer. *You* are the
painter.' To Jock Murray she wrote furiously: 'This seems
extremely cheap to me and brings this journey into the sort
of category I loathe ... anyway, as I have to do all the
talking, I am going to shunt all the business of food on to his
shoulders and shall jolly well make him too tired to write.'

The exchange set the tone for the trip. A jeep was hired,
with a driver called Ali whom Freya liked and cosseted and
Derek Hill thought a scoundrel; they got stuck repeatedly in
mud. The tent was rarely used, both travellers preferring
even the most primitive of hotels, and when it was, Freya
asked Derek Hill at breakfast why he hadn't shaved, an-
nouncing that in her day no gentleman would have
appeared before a lady unshaven. (Victorian England seldom
left Freya's side: when one night she found a two-and-a-
half-inch insect crawling along her thigh, she put on a
dressing gown and a 'boudoir' cap, before shouting for help.)
Seeking to make peace, Derek Hill asked her questions about
the battlefields through which they drove. 'Derek, I am not
your Cook's Tour.'

At Lake Van they parted, both falling with joy on Oleg
Polunin, who they found collecting flowers on the shore.
Freya was to go to Diyarbakir, Derek Hill to look at churches
in Ahtamar. 'I have been thinking about it, quite a lot,'

Freya remarked disingenuously to Jock Murray, 'and come to the conclusion that the tourist is content to *see* places, the traveller wants to *be* ... You must have guessed that I find Derek a tourist at heart and feel like strangling him at frequent intervals ... I left, with that wonderful feeling of exhilaration which seems to visit me when I drop a man.' Derek Hill was no less relieved. Though as admiring as ever of her sense of history and the infectious excitement with which she could conjure up a battle or a campaign, he had no talent for the role of courtier.

By the end of August, Freya was back in Asolo with a new book in mind, something to be easier than *Ionia*, a day-by-day travel book, following her progress along the west and south coasts of Turkey, then up through Alexander's battlefields. The reader, she told Jock Murray, might thus be led into Alexander with 'not too researchful wandering'.

Though she found starting a book painful, once into it she could write with extraordinary fluency, in spite of a houseful of guests, frequent breaks for visits to London (a 'sort of debutante season' as she described them aptly, for they included balls, country weekends and occasional meetings with the Queen Mother), having to make plans for future journeys, and her correspondence, important all her life, but never more so than in her later years.

Eight chapters into *The Lycian Shore*, she decided that Alexander needed a volume to himself, and was only slightly daunted to discover that most of her eighty-three research books were in German. As she worked her way into them, some of the characters she met seemed to her admirable;

others she despised. Soon they had become as familiar to her as a group of friends encountered during a London visit. 'Trajan,' she wrote to Jock Murray, 'I think is emerging as the central figure: he is not fascinating, like Hadrian, but he has all the *Western* typical virtues so that I think his very mistakes in the East should be of interest. And that tiresome conscientious Pliny was always asking him questions (must have been such a *bore* for him) which show the huge machine at work.' It might have been Hatfield House, over a long weekend.

There was something about the western and southern coasts of Turkey, with their remote valleys and treeless plateaux, that touched some chord in Freya. By 1956 she had made two long journeys, by horse and by jeep, feeling each time closer to the landscape and to the people among whom she was travelling. Her Turkish was improving. Antalya, far to the south, had become her base and she returned there each time with pleasure, to 'its outline of blue hills, a dark and fierce blue and so steep and tumbled'.

For the last major trip, in what had now become a three-part sequence of books, she accompanied Alexander along his route between Caria and Cilicia, trying as she went to understand why he should have chosen one path in prefer-ence to another, why he turned west, 'when his aim was all towards Gordium in the north'. On her donkey, in terrible weather, pausing on each hillside to stare and ponder, attempting to imagine Alexander and his men, Freya felt at her best. Letters to friends in London reflect her exhilaration. 'On the pass,' she wrote to Cockerell of her journey by horse past Mount Solyma, 'I had one of those good moments, a whole new slice of world opening below me – the wide valley of the Alaghir Chay, filled with small ranges and open places of its own and surrounded in the north by a bodyguard of high round hills still streaked with snow. What one feels most I think at such moments is the wonderful *variety* of the world.' The journey ended with a sea expedition to the headland round which Alexander was thought to have waded. Taking the daughter of her hotel-keeper with her, Freya put on her bathing suit and went round the cliff, swimming when it got too deep to stand.

Alexander's Path, her fourteenth book, was published in the autumn of 1958. On receiving the first copy, Freya commented that it looked alluring but that she was distressed to find it badly written, all except for the appendix. What she longed to do was to repunctuate it. Reviewers were rather kinder. In *The Times Literary Supplement*, the anonymous writer praised her for her contribution to history, for her superb prose style, 'rich yet never rococo', for her 'wise and luminous pages'. 'Miss Stark', he concluded, 'stands in an apostolic succession of great travel writers.'

Before the next year was over, Freya had found time to fit in one more quick book, *Riding to the Tigris*, the account of yet another journey, again on her own, through the Hakkiari mountains lying between Lake Van and the Tigris, the 'most rugged among the regions of Asia' as Canon Wigram, one of the rare travellers to reach there, had described them. Taking Lucullus as her guide, Freya got there too, by horse, despite dysentery and the police confiscating her photographs, noting with a touch of understandable self-satisfaction that she was probably the first Western woman to do so. She was in Trebizond when she heard that Nuri as-said Pasha, Prime Minister of Iraq and her friend from Baghdad days, had been murdered together with King Faisal and the ex-regent in a military coup. 'It makes seven of my friends or acquaintances murdered,' she wrote bleakly to Jock Murray, 'and Nuri I can't bear to think of . . . And I feel so deeply that we are to blame – for lack of vision, making it death to be our friend.' On her return to Europe, she was congratulated on her 'demure little notes on place names' that put to shame those responsible for the government maps.

It had been ten years of exceptionally hard work done in her late fifties and early sixties. Seven books, three of them volumes of autobiography, four of travel and history. Not surprising perhaps that Freya's versatility caused admiration. Was she historian, archaeologist, essayist or travel writer? Historians spoke kindly of her history, but dwelt with greater pleasure on her fine writing and artistic eye; archaeologists insisted that ruins were not her strong point, but that her sense of the characters in history was unmatched; some literary-minded academics praised her style, while others found it too dense, lacking the compelling sweep of strong narrative. In the general public and among her friends, there were those who preferred her essays, and others who, not always sharing her interpretations, found her vision, the way she related landscape and travel and people, beguiling, and were charmed by the way she treated moral qualities as if they were people. Everywhere, there was approval for her autobiography, and in particular the first volume, *Traveller's Prelude*, and high regard for her photographs, which caught so perfectly the barrenness and immensity of the landscapes she loved.

One of the few sour notes was cast only many years later, by the American critic Paul Fussell, who, writing of travel books, chose not to include her works on the grounds that in order to 'write a distinguished travel book you have to be equally interested in (1) the travel and (2) the writing', and that though Freya was unquestionably a traveller, 'the dimension of delight in language and disposition, in all the literary contrivances, isn't there'. If the judgement seemed harsh, and to many incorrect, it said much about the strength with which readers reacted to her work, and the different appeal it had for different people.

Sometime in the middle fifties, Freya discovered an enormous new pleasure: talking to and travelling with the young. It was not altogether new of course; in war-time Delhi, Baghdad and Cairo she had been much fêted by young soldiers on leave from the front. But this was something of her own. For about ten years, god-children, by this time reaching the age to appreciate her, and their friends were to become a central part of each year's plans. 'I am feeling old,' she wrote to Jock Murray as she departed one spring to see Alexander's northern passes, 'that is to say that I am just as ready to do things, but would like someone young to take on the unbelievable wear and tear of "getting a move on".'

Probably the first of Freya's young companions was Barclay Saunders, grand-daughter of Herbert Olivier, Robert Stark's friend in Paris in the 1890s. Freya had known her as a child at La Mortola, where Olivier had a house. In

1954 she asked whether she would like to accompany her around Sicily to look at ruins. Her intention was to relive the great marine battles of Syracuse, under Thucydides' direction, and to find a fisherman to row them round the harbour.

February had been chosen, for the blossom. Freya and Barclay Saunders reached Palermo in heavy rain. It was extremely cold. Wrapped up in mackintoshes over their tweeds, they travelled around the island by bus, staying at the cheapest *pensioni*, Freya worrying constantly about money. For lunch, they had picnics of doughnuts and oranges. At Syracuse, the rain was so persistent that they stood by the harbour wall, peering into almost invisible mist at an imaginary naval battle. It was some days before a fisherman could be persuaded to risk his rowing boat round the bay. Often wet, sometimes hungry, frequently kept awake at night by Freya's snores, Barclay Saunders remembers the journey with delight, as a moment of educational awakening.

Freya's travelling was always unpredictable, not least because she knew so many people. In Palermo, they called on the Lampedusas. *The Leopard* was written, but not yet published. At one of several feudal soirées, with Freya in long Arab dress, and flaming torches lighting up the immense Sicilian dining room, they were introduced to a young girl, the daughter of a neighbouring family, on whom *The Leopard*'s heroine Angelica had been modelled. The story of her unhappy love affair was recounted to Freya over dinner. Next morning, she told Barclay Saunders that she must invite the girl to London. (In due course, the girl arrived at Victoria Station, with her chaperone. She stayed just one night, and was so appalled by London that she caught the next boat-train back across the channel, after which she returned to Palermo to marry her lover.)

From this year on, young companions travelled everywhere with Freya. The role, older teacher to respectful pupil, was one she greatly preferred when on the move to the equivocating deliberations with equals. The long summer university holidays were ideal for Greek and Turkish expeditions, by bus, or one year, in comfort, minibus. At Ephesus, Troy, Didyma or Side, wide-brimmed hat sheltering her face, with stout shoes and lisle stockings, Freya would lean on a broken column and talk, describe events, recall episodes, quote perfectly from a dozen sources. The godsons, often classicists themselves, would listen and learn, and tend to the practical matters of travel; it was, remembers one, like 'travelling with your tutor', formidable, somewhat unnerving but always exhilarating. There was much laughter, of a rather high-minded sort. (After Barclay Saunders, of whom Freya was very fond, girls were never a great success. They seemed to Freya to lack the sensitivity and intelligence of the young men.)

In Asolo, in the Easter holidays, there might be reading parties, with everyone at work in a different corner of the house by day, gathering at six to play Scrabble and talk about life over a little vermouth by the library fire. Freya, sitting very upright, shoulders well back, rather small brown eyes very bright, needlework in her hand, would offer a theme: the nobility of military campaigning perhaps, or whether the Sumerians believed in an after-life. The godsons would be expected to take it up, competing a little among themselves. Casa Freia was a perfect setting for such occasions: the smell of wax from highly polished tile floors, the cabinets of coins and Roman pots, the dimly lit passages, the heavy striped silk curtains from the *tessoria* next door, all added to an air of serene scholarship, while the slight austerity in food and drink suited the spirit of Academe. It was order, of the right kind, intelligent, immutable, triumphing over the uneasy Bohemia of her childhood.

For Freya, these interludes did much to dispel loneliness. And she was immensely pleased when, as sometimes happened, she found someone who 'looked through the same window' and was fired by her own particular enthusiasms: both Malise Ruthven, son of Pamela Cooper, and Mark Lennox-Boyd, grandson of the Iveaghs she had known in Asolo as a girl, her most constant companions on her Turkish travels, chose to take up Arabic.

CHAPTER NINE

Montoria

Towards the end of April 1963, Jock Murray received a letter from Freya. 'The exciting news', she wrote, 'is that I have bought a little hill.' Driving one day with friends in search of land for them near Asolo she had been offered a steep grassy slope, some ten acres in all, with a view of other foothills all around, and a church and cypresses perched opposite. It was like no other landscape: a series of pointed molehills stretching out in front of the high Dolomites. She was enchanted with her purchase: a little wood at the bottom by a stream, some terraces, a small derelict cottage she hoped to build on to. Asolo itself had become too noisy; the moment had come to look for silence. Montoria, as the place was called, was to give Freya considerable pleasure; but it was also to torment her. All her life she had been exceptionally brave: over Montoria she almost lost her nerve.

Of the many sides of Freya's nature, the one that had least found expression in her wandering years had been her skills as a builder. Robert Stark, architect of houses she loved and gardens she remembered all her life, had bequeathed to her a strong feeling for stone and texture. Returning to Asolo in 1945 she had not hesitated about spending most of the war-reparation money on marble baths and basins, baroque fantasies of shells and scrolls. Later she had even designed for herself a revolving desk, twenty drawers and four niches covered in burgundy morocco with columns and brass capitals. But these were details. Montoria was an enormous undertaking. Freya was soon driving, in an unsuitable two-seater sky-blue open car that had captivated her, rather like Mr Toad, with its three hooters and leather seats, to stone quarries near Grappa in search of the perfect slab of marble for the window sills, stairs and swimming-pool border or to Bassano for a modern kitchen. Letters at this time are given over almost entirely to plans: shall the pool have rough stone or smooth? Where will its exit pipes run? Where should the asparagus bed be laid? Casa Freia, beloved for so many years by several generations of guests, was now on the market; the prospective buyers, Freya commented characteristically, were 'rather touching, all with money from industry and longing for culture so that I feel like one of those decayed Romans with the young and eager and uncouth barbarians pouring in'. With those who protested about losing the old house, she was firm.

The idea of building on to the existing cottage was quickly abandoned. Freya's designs, on paper, were grandiose and triumphant; the proportions palatial. Drawing rooms with magnificent vistas and parquet floors; more baroque porphyry bathrooms; room upon room for god-children, friends, passing scholars: Montoria grew and grew. Above the front door was placed a vast stone lintel: *'Noi siam pellegrini, come voi altri'* ('we are travellers, as you are').

Soon Freya was looking for friends to share it with her, to

occupy the ground floor while she took the first, and to inherit it after her death. For a while, it looked as if the Coopers might join her, then another newer friend, Dulcie Deuchar. Costs mounted and Freya, having trouble selling the old house, grew increasingly anxious. The *tessoria* was sold to Caroly Piaser and brought in a little money. Friends made loans; others were asked to take a gamble but no one could be found to take it on. 'I am so demoralized by the unreliability of most of my friends,' she noted, desperately but somewhat unreasonably. A project started with confidence and promise grew sour. Serious financial disaster was halted in the end only when a tenant, a retired QC called David Karmel, offered £1,000 a year in rent for the ground floor.

The year of the house, Freya had turned seventy. She was not in London for her birthday, so Jock Murray promised a celebration the following January. As the day grew closer it was clear there was going to be a problem about numbers. Who, among Freya's considerable list of distinguished friends, could be excluded? It was solved, quite simply, by eliminating women. Seton Lloyd, Lord David Cecil, the Earl of Euston, Michael Stewart, Harold Caccia, John Sparrow, Patrick Kinross, Gordon Waterfield and a selection of the young, sixteen men and Freya, gathered in a private room in a hotel for dinner. Freya wore white, and circulated. The birthday, she remarked afterwards, could not have been better planned.

It was not that Freya was without women friends. As she had observed in 1938, after her months with Gertrude Caton Thompson in the Hadhramaut, 'I had begun to think . . . that I might be one of those women who hate other women and are only easy with men: but I now realized that what I dislike is the arrogance of the unfeminine women, neither one thing nor the other. The lovely and the brilliant or good of my own sex, Celia Johnson, Biddy Carlisle, Phyllis Balfour, Virginia Woolf, Dora Gordine and many others, I met and admired and easily love – great people all moving like queens in their own atmosphere, and none of them, it suddenly strikes me, fond of working on committees.' Women were not, however, as cosy as men in Freya's eyes, nor as intellectual, and for this kind of occasion, most definitely not as much fun. (Wives were never much fun; of those she despised, or found vacillating or tiresome, Freya could be extremely dismissive.)

The early sixties continued to be years of exceptional activity. Montoria took a great deal of time; friends, several of whom had also bought plots of land and built around Montoria, and social life almost as much, though many of her wartime friends were now dead, and she reported mournfully that she had just written her tenth letter of condolence in five months. These deaths greatly saddened Freya; they reminded her of what very good times there had been. But they did not depress her, nor was she ever sentimental about death in the way she could be about royalty or soldiers. She seldom went to funerals, even of those very close to her, saying that they made her 'feel like walking behind a used-up dress however loved'.

Freya was also occupied with what was to be the last of her major books. Alexander, her companion for eight years, had finally receded. She had turned her attention to the Romans, and to their frontier wars along the Euphrates.

The idea, she explained, had come to her because 'I grew up near a frontier, and learned to trespass across it (and a good many others) in my time: and the impediment which it produces in human intercourse has always seemed to me a historical monstrosity.' The book was intended to be short, but eight centuries of Roman history demanded much research, and when Freya was not deliberating between Carrara marble and travertine stone, she was deep and not always approvingly at work among people who like all her historical characters were rapidly assuming the personalities of men met at a bad dinner party. 'I must try', she wrote to Jock Murray, 'and find a few nice ones to keep me going; Pliny so boring, Cicero insufferable, Julian, I discover on reading his letters, an appalling prig. Even Catullus jeers at a man *for being poor*! What a relief to turn to Polybius who was a Greek. I would have liked to marry him. What a *decent* person.' To test her theory that the Roman Empire had disintegrated because its frontier was too long to defend easily, she now fitted in a new round of journeys, travelling at one point down a gorge for ten days on a donkey.

When *Rome of the Euphrates* appeared it was neither short, nor an easy read, assuming considerable background knowledge in its readers. One reviewer remarked that 'if Herodotus had been a woman and an artist with a camera, this is the sort of book he might have written'. Freya was delighted, for not all were as kind.

Freya's poor health, so destructive of her plans when young, returned to plague her in later life. Sinus, cataracts, sciatica, a bad hip; one followed the other. She dealt with them as she had dealt with typhoid, dengue fever and dysentery, without complaint, holding court from hospital beds in négligé and lace cap, preferring always Thucydides to questions as to how she felt, and using the enforced idleness rather pleasurably to answer for herself such troubling moral questions as whether or not she believed that moral virtues kept 'their timeless divinity across the border'. To Lady Cholmondeley, after a hip operation, she reported: 'I am also trying now to do little *jumps* from one carpet to the next (alas, I was once described as a beautiful *leaping* creature!).'

In her seventies, no more than in her thirties, would she permit physical frailty to stand between her and travel. It was simply a matter of arranging things in such a way that she could manage. Shortly after her seventy-fifth birthday, she told Pam Cooper that she considered her requirements for the next ten years to be: '(1) travel in greater comfort: no more of those happy trips third class in steamers; (2) provide for illness; (3) eventually, in my case, probably pay for someone to travel with me (poor thing); (4) be able to afford short jaunts for fun ... (5) most of all, be able to have friends rather than tenants in the bottom flat.'

In the summers, Freya continued to go to the coast of Turkey or Greece to swim, almost always stopping off at some point at Kardamyli, in the Peloponnese, to stay with Patrick Leigh Fermor. In the spring and autumn came the more ambitious journeys, to Peking, to visit the Stewarts at the embassy, to Persia, the Yemen, Tunisia, Austria, the Middle East, wherever there were friends who offered beds and trips into the desert or up into the mountains, occasions which Freya, so knowledgeable and so obviously enjoying herself, made fun. In July 1968 she was in Kabul, preparing to cross Afghanistan from east to west in a Land-Rover, travelling from six in the morning until five at night. Less than a year later, it was Persepolis, Isfahan, Nishapur and Pasargadee with Lady Cholmondeley. Both women were in their late seventies. Freya was stern about when they should and should not wear veils. Searching for a caravanserai too close to the Russian border they were arrested and, since they had left their passports in their hotel in Meshed, held by a garrison until a British consular official could be found to bail them out. Freya, able all her life to fall asleep instantly wherever she was, chose a bench and slept the hours away. On their release, they pressed on to see the ruin they had come to visit, Freya remarking how much finer it was in the late afternoon light, among the shining poppies. The taxi driver had long since given up; it was Lady Cholmondeley who drove them back to Meshed.

On all these journeys, Freya shopped: statues, coins, jewellery, carpets. Friends detailed to meet her at European airports on her return would watch appalled as this small figure, clothed in the most brilliant and visible of outfits, a bunch of bright parasols tucked under her arm, would totter across the tarmac, plainly laden down with packages of rare antiquities, her jacket bulging with bales of silk wrapped around her middle, a false-bottomed bag jangling with undeclared objects. Customs officials proved as gullible, or as charmed, as they had in Ventimiglia in the twenties. The trophies took their place in the marble niches and shelves of Montoria.

Freya had never stopped preferring mountains. In the

spring of 1969 she heard of an ex-colonel in the Gurkhas who organized expeditions around the skirts of Everest and Annapurna. Six years beyond his age limit, unable as she confessed to walk at all far, she wrote to ask him whether a pony could be arranged. He replied suggesting Annapurna, and promised a mount. Freya took Mark Lennox-Boyd with her. Camping at 9,000 feet, looking out over three peaks of Annapurna, Freya wrote of the 'awe and majesty of this approach, the last terrestrial footsteps to infinity'. It was here, she told him, that she would really like to die. Mountains reminded her of faith. 'I sit in the shadows,' she would say, 'but I look at the light.'

Early in 1971, Freya began sorting through her letters. It was a vast and time-consuming process for she had been writing steadily for over sixty years, sometimes as many as ten letters a day. Having issued instructions to friends ever since the twenties to keep the originals she now wrote to them to call them back; bundles containing sometimes several hundred letters, a firm scrawl on thin blue airmail paper, now began reaching Montoria. Other travellers have kept diaries; Freya had chosen to set down the record of her life in letters, using them as touchstone for the volumes of autobiography and the travel books to come. Sir Sydney Cockerell, with Jock Murray the closest of her literary advisers, had been given a selection to read as early as 1938. 'Magnanimous, vivid, picturesque, closely observant of men and things,' he wrote in his own diary, 'and written with an easy mastery that is never forced and that will make them a very precious record in days to come.'

That day seemed to Freya to have arrived. As she read back, she was struck by the sheer amount of historical detail contained in their pages. The span of her life alone, she wrote to Lord David Cecil, made them valuable. 'What I feel most strongly is that we lived in what was, after all, a heroic age: St Crispin didn't find us in bed; and that is a deep happiness.' There was too, of course, an element of self-revelation: 'The interest or main line is not in the war,' she noted, 'but in the almost Tolstoyan development of a human being in extraordinary family relationships . . . My journeys, and even my writing, are really the consequences and secondary to this grinding of my youth.'

Shrewd as she was about contracts and royalties, Freya was never greatly in tune with the financial realities of the publishing world. Having what she took to be an extraordinary and possibly unique chronicle of contemporary life in her hands she envisaged it quite simply as a 'Murray classic' running to at least six volumes, possibly more, the letters published in their near entirety. The exchanges that now followed with Jock Murray showed just how very stubborn she could be. Freya had fought with him over the mink coat; over Gertrude Caton Thompson; over cuts to *Dust in the Lion's Paw*, when she accused him of thinking that she had 'a servant-hall taste for grandeur'. The most bitter battle was over the letters. Six volumes were not financially viable, and Jock Murray was forced to tell her so. Her reaction arrived in the next post. 'Your little note comes just after my long letter went, and it upset me so much I was *sick*.' There was, she declared, no question at all of a selection.

Michael Russell, a small publisher, was eventually found

to take on what in the end turned into eight volumes of letters. All were from Freya, to her mother, and to the friends and acquaintances of over seventy years. As she explained to Paul Scott, who became a new correspondent after an enthusiastic review of the first volume in *Country Life*: 'I have been so much alone that it has gradually become my easiest way of conversation – one has intervals to think over whatever the subject may have been and presently the pleasantest of patterns shapes itself, a little bit from each side and gradually the shape of its own emerging.' Though never commercial as a venture, the letters found favour with reviewers. The travel books had presented a rounded picture, distanced by memory; it is the letters that give the feel of travel, with its confusions, pleasures, anxieties; those who read them were taken by the vision, the great sweep that seemed to encompass 2,000 years of civilization, and were charmed by the traveller and her humour. Freya, by now also working on a new selection of essays, 'an *old* version of *Perseus*, all on age and death but not I think depressing' (to be called, she suggested, like the chocolates, *After Eighty*), watched over their reception with a satisfaction she had not felt for years. It was matched perhaps only by the delight of being made a Dame in the New Year Honours List of 1972. She found the title, she told friends, austere; in Italy she would stick to 'Donna'.

In her seventies and eighties Freya lost none of her attention to world events, particularly in the Near East which in letters to *The Times* she was able to suggest were merely consequences of earlier unfortunate policies, nor did she relinquish her fondness for Empire nor her capacity to be absurd about it. To Paul Scott, after enjoying his *Raj Quartet*, she wrote: 'I wondered whether the clue to our failure (in India) could not be found in the different system on which civil and military seemed to work. I thought the army was still wanted but practically everyone wished the civilians to go (1945), and was it because the army was *paternal?* I wondered whether a *deification* of the Viceroy and his wife could not have served the British rule?' Nor was her particular form of sharpness muted. People she had not liked earlier in life were unlikely to find her more yielding now. Discovering herself at a dinner in London to be seated near Mountbatten, with whom she had scored so little success in Delhi, she remarked that he was 'not inspired, and rather disintegrated like that beautiful profile of his'. She greatly preferred Sir Francis Chichester, seated on her other side, with whom she had a 'splendid talk of deserts and seas, like tumbling suddenly into the Elizabethan age'. Invited to the Huxleys' golden wedding, she wrote: 'Fifty years of looking after Julian! Juliette should appear with a palm branch in her hand like one of those Byzantine martyrs.' And it was really to Freya that went the last word on Gertrude Caton Thompson. Urged to be charitable when volume three of the letters, dealing with the Hadhramaut, was being prepared, Freya jibbed. It was pointed out that the archaeologist was, after all, still alive. 'Typical,' said Freya.

In the late seventies came two more journeys. The BBC had asked Freya whether she would like to make an expedition in the Near East with a film crew. She chose a stretch of the Euphrates she had seen first almost fifty years earlier, when she had admired rafts carrying wood down from Turkey to sell in Iraq, and longed to commandeer her own, pausing to take to a horse when a castle appeared on the horizon. Mark Lennox-Boyd and his wife Arabella were invited to join the party. To the director, Freya sent off notes about how she envisaged the scenes. There would be, she thought, '*conversation* as the landscape went by, pointing at this and that as it caught our eye . . .' In order to slip them casually into her talk, Freya now set about boning up on Trajan and the Battle of Carrhae and preparing outfits suitable for raft life. The expedition took place in May 1977. Beset by problems of timing, by a new dam that had completely altered the river and its purpose since Freya first cast eyes on it, by near war between Syria and Iraq and by the raft itself, built more as prop than functioning boat, it was not a total success. Freya loved it – though she worried that she might not appear at her best, since she 'never wore make-up on a raft' – and said she would travel to the Middle East whenever she was asked and had the strength.

Soon afterwards, she went to practise riding on a pony on Dartmoor, and returned to trek around Annapurna. Freya was now eighty-six. Dick Waller, son of her friend Dorothy, with whom she had cantered across the Devonshire moors at seventeen talking about socialism, was worried about her strength. Helped up on to her pony the first day in India, Freya trotted briskly off and up a pass and out of sight; two hours later, on foot, panting and deeply anxious, he caught up with her. 'I just wanted, dear, to show you I could still do it.' In the days that followed there were evenings when, after seven hours on her pony, Freya was too stiff to move, and had to be lifted off and carried into her tent. She never referred to it.

In 1973 Freya sold Montoria. Financially it had never been anything but disastrous, with debt piling on debt. The recession, the lira, the exchange rate had all been against her. The garden, and in particular its roses, had given her pleasure, as had the splendour and proportions of her great house. It went to a bicycle-saddle maker from the Veneto. With the money, Freya moved to a flat in Asolo, with a view across the valley to the Dolomites: the books, the pictures, the coins and statues and the old silks from the *tessoria* went with her, as did one ornate marble bath. 'I am dead tired and feel too old for these gymnastics,' she complained to Jock Murray. Almost at once, however, she was enjoying the rearranging, and protested strongly when he spoke of envying the young: 'You say one should try not to – but I can't imagine doing so. It would be *awful* to go back when one is so much nearer to the goal . . . I feel about it as about the first ball, or the first meet of hounds, anxious as to whether one will get it right, and timid and inexperienced – all the feelings of youth.' What was more, she had a new car, always something that delighted her, in the shape of a Dormobile, one she had coveted for years and that came to her as a present from a new friend, Anita Forrer. Perched on the high seat, her short legs barely reaching the pedals, her travelling companions reduced most often to speechless apprehension, she took it off for jaunts up the winding mountain passes and into the Dolomites. Not until she reached eighty-two was Freya finally persuaded to part with it.

On 26 May 1984 Freya was presented with the keys to Asolo. To the ceremony, attended by friends and the entire village, came the Blues and Royals, the band of the Household Cavalry. All morning, the rain poured down. At two o'clock, as they piped and drummed, wheeling and forming up and down the Piazza to music chosen by her, the sky cleared. To Freya, so charmed by pageantry, so approving of soldiers, it was a splendid sight.

While in Aden in 1940, Freya Stark began a series of long auto-biographical letters to Sir Sydney Cockerell. Completed during subsequent breaks in her war work, they covered several hundred typed pages, describing her life up to 1944. In 1948, married and living in Asolo, she used these letters as the basis of one of the most enjoyable of all contemporary autobiographies, *Traveller's Prelude*; over the next twelve years followed three more volumes; *Beyond Euphrates*, *The Coast of Incense* and *Dust in the Lion's Paw*.

Of all the twentieth-century travellers and writers, Freya Stark's life is possibly one of the best and most fully documented. She was an excellent and exceptionally conscientious letter writer, both to her family and to a small group of friends – Bernard Berenson, Sir Sydney Cockerell, Field Marshal Wavell and Jock Murray, her life-long publisher – to whom she wrote, often almost daily. Between 1974 and 1982 appeared eight volumes of these letters (published by Michael Russell Ltd), starting from when she was twenty-one at the outbreak of the First World War and ending in 1980, when she was eighty-seven. They give a remarkable picture of practically the whole of this century, with their huge cast of characters, from travellers to statesmen, diplomats to politicians; they are also a unique personal chronicle of a traveller's life that is both funny and intimate.

Before the war, Freya Stark travelled in the Near East; after it, through Asia Minor. Her accounts of these journeys, exceptional

in their detail and ability to relate landscape, people and history, interweave past with present, knowledge with observation. There are ten books of travel spaced over
thirty-five years; not as easy as the more personal accounts, they are companions with which to journey and observe.

The first of them, *The Valleys of the Assassins*, an account of two early journeys across Persia in search of lost treasure and unmapped castles, was embarked on, as she writes in the preface, 'single-mindedly for fun'; much of that enjoyment, the delight in discovery and intense pleasure in solitude, comes across in its pages. Among the post-war books, there is *Ionia, a Quest*, a scholarly 'guide-book in time', written after visiting fifty-five ruined sites along the western coast of Asia Minor. The two books, written with twenty years between them, both contain an easy blending of time and place, and the same considered pauses for reflection.

To these two sets of books can be added two more; the collections of photographs and the essays. From her first days as a traveller in the East, Freya Stark took photographs; they are of people and of places and many were taken at a time when no one else had travelled in these regions before. They appear as illustrations in the travel books and on their own, in separate collections. As for the essays, she began her observation of human behaviour, frailties, tastes and qualities in her thirties; they have formed the basis of a number of distinctive and pleasurable volumes of what she once referred to as her 'own Everywoman philosophy' and of which the first, *Perseus in the Wind*, remains the most outstanding.

All Freya Stark's books are in print in Great Britain, published by John Murray. Century have published several of them in paperback including *Traveller's Prelude* and *Perseus in the Wind*. Her books are published in the USA by Transatlantic.